The Thoreau

Centennial

Bust of HENRY DAVID THOREAU *by Malvina Hoffman*
(Unveiled at the Hall of Fame, New York University, May 6, 1962)

The Thoreau Centennial

PAPERS MARKING THE OBSERVANCE IN NEW YORK CITY OF THE ONE HUNDRETH ANNIVERSARY OF THE DEATH OF HENRY DAVID THOREAU

Edited by

WALTER HARDING

STATE UNIVERSITY OF NEW YORK PRESS

A careful effort has been made to trace the ownership of selections included in this book in order to secure permission to reprint copyright material and to make full acknowledgment of their use. Specific references to material used appear at the bottom of appropriate pages within the text. If any error or omission has occurred, it is purely inadvertent and will be corrected in subsequent editions, provided written notification is made to the publisher.

FOR

LEWIS LEARY

who was the guiding spirit of the
Thoreau Centennial Meetings

Contents

Introduction

The papers gathered in this volume were among those delivered at the Thoreau Centennial meetings at the Pierpont Morgan Library, the Community Church, and New York University's Hall of Fame in New York City on May 5 and 6, 1962, under the sponsorship of the Thoreau Society, and under the leadership of Professor Lewis Leary of Columbia University, then President of the Thoreau Society. The wide variety in subject and approach of these papers is in itself ample indication of Thoreau's multifaceted appeal today. Here we find an internationally known statesman from India, one of New York City's leading clergymen, and college professors from as diverse points as North Carolina, Texas, and Vermont —each paying his tribute in his own way.

Professor Carl F. Hovde, Associate Professor of English at Columbia University, who did his doctoral dissertation at Princeton University on Thoreau's *Week,* here studies Thoreau's conception of character in his first book in the light of the revisions of his manuscripts. A novelist friend of mine thought Thoreau was so adept at character creation in his travel essays that she lamented the fact that he had never written any fiction. Mr. Hovde demonstrates not only the care with which Thoreau reworked his books but why character development was always secondary to theme in his writings—and thus, indirectly, why Thoreau was never tempted to turn to the writing of fiction.

In recent years—the turning point probably came with the publication of F. O. Matthiessen's seminal *American Renaissance* in 1941—there has been a growing interest in Thoreau as a literary stylist and in his use of imagery and figurative language. This interest is reflected in this volume by Joseph J. Moldenhauer's paper. Mr. Moldenhauer is Assistant Professor of English at the University of Texas.

1

Walter Harding's "The Last Days of Henry Thoreau" is an adaptation of the closing chapter of his forthcoming biography of Thoreau, a study which unlike earlier biographies of Thoreau aims at a presentation rather than an interpretation of the facts. Mr. Harding is Chairman of the English Department of the State University College at Geneseo, New York, and Secretary of the Thoreau Society.

Thoreau's present stature and fame are the product of a comparatively recent surge of interest in his life and writings. In his own day and for many years thereafter he was most generally dismissed as a second-rate disciple and imitator of Ralph Waldo Emerson. It is particularly appropriate that the account of the turn in Thoreau's reputation is told by Raymond Adams, Professor of English at the University of North Carolina, and the dean of the present generation of Thoreau scholars.

Were the last years of Thoreau's life an anticlimax? Was he disillusioned and disappointed with life? Many critics and biographers of Thoreau have answered "Yes" to those questions, but J. Lyndon Shanley, Professor of English at Northwestern University, former President of the Thoreau Society, and author of *The Making of Walden,* has re-examined the facts and in "Thoreau: Years of Decay and Disappointment?" comes up with a resounding "No!"

Reginald L. Cook, Chairman of the American Literature Department at Middlebury College, Director of the Breadloaf School of English, and author of *Passage to Walden,* as the result of a lifelong study of Thoreau and a friendship of many years' standing with Robert Frost, has demonstrated in "A Parallel of Parablists" the affinities of two of our greatest American authors.

Howard Mumford Jones, Professor Emeritus of English at Harvard University, in "Thoreau and Human Nature," examines Thoreau as an aphorist and a moralist in the light of a close reading of his *Journal.*

Rev. Donald S. Harrington, minister of the Community

Church in New York City, in his sermon "Living Is So Dear" discusses Thoreau's philosophy as a guide for life today.

Raymond Adams, in "Thoreau's Claim to Greatness," discusses why Thoreau, a century after his death, was finally chosen for inclusion in the Hall of Fame.

And in the closing paper, His Excellency Braj Kumar Nehru, Ambassador to the United States from India, in recognition of Thoreau's world-wide influence and particularly of his influence on one of the greatest men of our century, Mahatma Gandhi, pays tribute to Thoreau.

The papers by Mr. Hovde, Mr. Moldenhauer, Mr. Harding, Mr. Shanley, and Mr. Cook were delivered at the sessions held in the Morgan Library on Saturday, May 5, 1962. Mr. Adams' first paper and Mr. Jones' paper were given at the Community Church of New York City on May 5th. Mr. Harrington's paper was the Sunday morning sermon at Community Church on May 6th. And Mr. Adams' second paper and Ambassador Nehru's tribute were delivered at the ceremonies dedicating Malvina Hoffman's bust of Thoreau at New York University's Hall of Fame on May 6th.

These meetings were held to commemorate the centennial of Thoreau's death. Similar meetings were held in Concord, Massachusetts; Washington, D. C.; Logan, Utah; Detroit, Michigan; and Tokyo, Japan. To most of Thoreau's contemporaries that such a series of meetings should be held a century later would have seemed almost inconceivable. Yet such has been the growth of Thoreau's reputation, that we can fully expect his bicentennial to be even more widely observed.

It has taken Henry David Thoreau a full century to attain his present high peak of fame and honor, but from the wide range of this collection of papers we can see how diversified that fame is. He is honored as a writer, as the creator of some of the most powerful, most effective prose in our language, and as the author of one of the truly great classics of American literature, *Walden*. He is honored as a naturalist, as the inventor of the natural history essay, as the recorder of the ways of the flora and fauna of his native Concord—from man to moss. He is honored as a political theorist and his essay on "Civil Disobedience" has had repercussions from South Africa to India, from Copenhagen, Denmark, to Montgomery, Alabama. He is honored as a critic of the foibles and follies of the complex ways of our modern life where status-seeking has become more important than soul-searching and we find ourselves living everyone's life but our own. But, above all, he is honored as a Transcendentalist—as a spiritual pioneer who points the way to a better life and as one who is certain, that if we but work for it, we can attain that better life here on earth.

I wish to express my appreciation to the various individuals who have prepared their papers for this volume and to the various periodicals for permission to reprint those papers which have already appeared in their pages. I wish also to thank the staffs of the Morgan Library, the Community Church of New York City, and the New York University Hall of Fame for their part in sponsoring the meetings, and to the Thoreau Society Centennial Committee—Mr. Brooks Atkinson, Mr. Theodore L. Bailey, Professor John Broderick, the Reverend Donald S. Harrington, Mrs. Herbert B. Hosmer, Mr. Leonard F. Kleinfeld, Mr. Milton Meltzer, Mrs. Caleb Wheeler, and Professor Lewis Leary, Chairman—for its part in the preparation for the meetings.

WALTER HARDING, *Secretary*
The Thoreau Society

State University College
Geneseo, New York
September 27, 1963

CARL HOVDE

The Conception of Character in

"A WEEK ON THE

CONCORD AND MERRIMACK RIVERS"

In one of the manuscripts for *A Week on the Concord and Merrimack Rivers,* Thoreau recorded several anecdotes about his grandmother. These stories were intended for the chapter entitled "Wednesday;" one of them concerns the effects produced by a new buggy the family had acquired, and describes the excitement caused by his grandmother's appearance in this vehicle.

Her chaise so frightened the geese in the road that they actually rose and flew half a mile, and sheep all ran over the hills, with the pigs after them and some of the horses they met broke their tackling or threw their riders, so that they had to put their chaise down several times to save life, and when they drove up to the meeting-house, snap, snap went the bridles of every one of the horses that were tied there, and they scattered without a benediction and though it was in the middle of the sermon time the whole congregation rushed out.[1]

There is more of this, and it is a fairly amusing story—vivid and colorful, and exactly the sort of intimate family detail so rare in Thoreau's writings. And yet, Thoreau

[1] HM 13195. I wish to thank the Director and Librarian of the Huntington Library, San Marino, California, for permission to examine and quote from two manuscripts in the collection—HM 956 and HM 13195.

5

rejected this story; it is not in the final version of the book, from which, indeed, the grandmother has disappeared altogether. One wonders at first why he chose to omit such promising material—and this example is only one among many. To pose questions about the reason for these changes is finally to wonder about the way Thoreau handles his characters in the book. He is clearly selective in his use of detail, and one may fairly say that his conception of character is deliberately limited when compared with the wide range of possibilities we see in *Walden*.

A Week on the Concord is, of course, Thoreau's first book, published five years before *Walden;* like that famous later work, it is based upon personal experience. After an introductory essay, "Concord River," where he treats the river as a stream which moistens and fructifies both the surrounding countryside and a sensitive man's imagination, he gives the basic biographical facts at the beginning of "Saturday," the first proper chapter, and the beginning of the week he was to spend on his trip.

> At length, on Saturday, the last day of August, 1839, we two, brothers, and natives of Concord, weighed anchor in this river port; for Concord, too, lies under the sun . . . one shore at least exempted from all duties but such as an honest man will gladly discharge. A warm, drizzling rain had obscured the morning, and threatened to delay our voyage, but at length the leaves and grass were dried, and it came out a mild afternoon, as serene and fresh as if Nature were maturing some greater scheme of her own. After this long dripping and oozing from every pore, she began to respire again more healthily than ever. So with a vigorous shove we launched our boat from the bank, while the flags and bulrushes courtesied a God-speed, and dropped silently down the stream.[2]

Thoreau begins the paragraph with specific personal information, moves on to the generalized significance of

---

[2] Henry David Thoreau, *The Writings of Henry David Thoreau*, Walden Edition, 20 vols. (Boston, 1906), I, p. 12. Hereafter cited as *A Week*.

Concord's being a "port of entry and departure for the bodies as well as the souls of men," goes on to place man, and Concord, firmly in the free and generous life of Nature, and then returns, at the end, to the specific occasion for the trip that he and his brother John took in the summer of 1839.

The paragraph is a kind of view in miniature of how *A Week on the Concord* is organized. The movement from particular fact, to that fact's general significance, and back again, is of course a very common movement in Thoreau's prose. But how solidly are we back at the level of autobiographical detail when he is describing the voyage? Every reader of *A Week* notices that Henry's brother John is never closely identified: he is never named; we are never told of his individual actions or thoughts; he simply does not exist in the work as a personality. He is a presence only, whose literary function is to provide that sense of companionship and joint enterprise creatable by the first person plural pronoun. He is, then, a representative companion, whose individual identity is of minimal significance.

There are, of course, many particular people mentioned in the work, and we do learn a good deal about some of them, but almost all of them are present to stand for certain qualities and attributes in a representative way; Thoreau often takes pleasure in their particularity, but is at pains to use them to show something about the general possibilities of man's spirit. And in *A Week* these possibilities are almost always positive—are good; this is a contrast with the vivid awareness of evil characteristic of the early part of *Walden*. *Walden* opens with perhaps the most brilliantly surgical scorn in American literature. It begins with a portrait of the worst of man's habits, which are even more frightening than profound evil because so much more common, and the work moves on to a presentation of what the best life must involve, wherever it may be lived. But *A Week* has neither the scorn, nor the deep penetration into the single self that is the purpose of *Walden*. In the earlier work many people are mentioned, but none of them is dwelled on very long, and while we are constantly hearing the sound of Thoreau's own voice, there is not the same deep delving into the biographical springs of personality.

The reason for this is reflected in the different evocations of Nature in the two works, for Nature is, of course, where Thoreau saw the roots of a man's proper character finding nourishment. In *Walden*, after the initial dissection of man's folly, we see Thoreau investigating himself, and at length, within the life of Nature as it existed at and around the pond. It is a confrontation of the individual with the ground of his very existence; he is much alone, though never lonely, because his enterprise is one that demands solitude for observation and for thought. This is one of the reasons for the great solitudes and silences of *Walden;* they are there so that a man may think about what he essentially is. Nature in *Walden* is never empty, but for Thoreau's imaginative purpose it must be largely uninhabited.

About *A Week*, on the other hand, one wishes to use not so much the word "nature" as the word "landscape." *Walden* does not present a panoramic view of the surroundings because there is too intense an investigation into the local particularities. But in *A Week* there are many visual sweeps, covering much territory; Thoreau moves down reaches of the river, and we have a sense of long lawns and prospects, but not of profound retreats or of vast silences—despite a passage on silence at the end of the work.

We do not have these because the enterprise is different; Thoreau is here not searching for the springs of individual identity in all its complexity, but is, on the level of the physical voyage, surveying the bright, ideal surface of much human experience—an experience achieved by men living together in the communities of towns and villages. Nature is here not the setting for the transformation of one man's soul, but is the background for a frieze of figures, whose particular members are mentioned briefly in order to exemplify, rapidly and without travail, some of the many ways in which men may be identified as worthy. There are men and women almost always in view, or held in the memory, and they are often the dignitaries in the history of the towns which the brothers passed on the rivers. From local histories, and especially from the *New England Gazetteer*[3]—the work actually carried on the 1839 trip—Thoreau learned of the most solid men and women of the New England past, and set down the deeds of some of them as genuine heroes of their place and time. For Thoreau they were all the more appealing for being provincial. These characters are often treated with a deliberate and humorous distance, but it is a very mild irony, affectionate and admiring, always in tune with the positive, enriching possibilities of man's spirit that form the subjects of *A Week*.

The characters of *A Week* are hence representative men in miniature, so to say, and going back to Thoreau's grandmother and her chaise, one can be reasonably sure that he omitted her because the tales about her did not make her sufficiently an *exemplum* for his exposition of a moral meaning; the incident was diverting, but not much more. The change he made in material about a man who does appear in the final version of the book provides another illustration of Thoreau's drive for the general and representative rather than the intensely particular and individual. In "Wednesday" again, he is describing some of the distinguished early settlers of several New England towns. He remarks that "Every town which we passed, if

[3] John Hayward, *The New England Gazetteer* (6th ed., Concord, N.H. and Boston, 1839).

we may believe the Gazeteer, had been the residence of some great man."[4]

In the finished book we find a discussion of John Stark, of Manchester, New Hampshire, and learn that he was

a hero of two wars, and survivor of a third, and at his death the last but one of the American generals of the Revolution. He was born in the adjoining town of Londonderry, then Nutfield, in 1728. As early as 1752, he was taken prisoner by the Indians while hunting in the wilderness near Baker's River; he performed notable service as a captain of rangers in the French war; commanded a regiment of the New Hampshire militia at the battle of Bunker Hill; and fought and won the battle of Bennington in 1777. He was past service in the last war, and died here in 1822, at the age of ninty-four. His monument stands upon the second bank of the river, about a mile and a half above the falls, and commands a prospect several miles up and down the Merrimack. It suggested how much more impressive in the landscape is the tomb of a hero than the dwellings of the inglorious living. Who is most dead,—a hero by whose monument you stand, or his descendants of whom you have never heard?[5]

Thoreau is here reviewing the peaks of Stark's achievement; his main accomplishments are there, none of them is dwelled upon, and the effect of this rapid list is to portray a man of affairs and a hero in almost generic terms—something Thoreau stressed by ending with a comparison of a hero's tomb and the anonymity of his descendants.

In an earlier manuscript version of this passage, Thoreau had gone into greater detail. He wrote of Stark that

when a prisoner among the Indians, being compelled to run the gauntlet, he snatched a club from the nearest one, and laying it lustily about him, by his courage and activity escaped almost without a blow, greatly to the delight of the old men of the tribe who were looking on. When set

[4] A Week, p. 169.
[5] Ibid., pp. 168–169.

to hoe corn by them, understanding well the Indian character, he took care not to exhibit any skill in this labor, to
which he had no doubt been accustomed on his father's
farm, but cut up the corn and left the weeds, and when
this did not release him, he threw his hoe into the river
declaring that "it was the business not of warriors, but of
Squaws, to hoe corn." This conduct at length gained him
the respect of the Indians, and the title of young chief,
with the honor of adoption into the tribe.[6]

This detail about the Indians is perfectly possible material,
of course, as it has all of the moral significance which
the story of the grandmother's buggy lacked. But it would
have caused Thoreau to linger over Stark longer than he
wished; in the final text, Stark is only one dignitary mentioned among many, and a larger passage would have
been out of proportion. The wish was not to dwell quite
so much on the individual accomplishment for its own
sake, but to present just enough particular detail to give
body to a recital of the heroes; comments from the
Gazetteer serve as ballast here, to make these figures stable
and significant, but it is the public and not the private
face that is being sketched. Stark takes his place as one
figure in a frieze portraying diverse fulfillments. He is
given enough individuality to make us believe in him, and
no more; it is the hero's tomb which dominates the scene,
throwing its shadow on the present.

This drive toward the positive and exemplary is reflected
in the relative scarcity of unfavorable, or negative, comment and criticism in *A Week*, something already mentioned as a contrast to the early parts of *Walden*. Take
the matter of slavery, for example. It is very likely that
at one time Thoreau intended to include in *A Week*—in
the chapter called "Thursday"—a version of an essay he
had written about Nathaniel P. Rogers, the abolitionist
who published a paper called *The Herald of Freedom*.

⁶ HM 13195.

The essay had been printed in the *Dial* in 1844, and manuscript evidence suggests that Thoreau tried to rework it for *A Week*. But he rejected it because it was so much concerned with social criticism. Rogers' paper was founded to oppose slavery, a particular social abuse, and the little social criticism to be found in *A Week* is very carefully stated in general terms. Often, of course, Thoreau strikes out against those things in public life to which he objects, but he almost never does this with reference to particular evils. He mentions slavery only once in the book, but does not dwell on it, and the tone of the sentence where it appears is one of criticism in the abstract. The paper on Rogers drops out because *A Week* is not meant to be a social document in the sense that "Civil Disobedience" is one, or even in the subtle fashion of parts of *Walden*. There are other passages in the manuscript which were omitted for similar reasons. Thus one sees him cutting out entirely not only passages which seemed to be morally unprofitable, like that on his grandmother, but also others which seemed too moral, so to say—passages which were out of harmony with the generally affirmative tone of his work.

Thoreau often "revised by omission" in this way, but his craftsmanship is more subtly demonstrated in those reworkings of earlier material which actually changed the report of what he saw in order to make reality better serve his own ends. In "Tuesday," Thoreau tells of a stop he made, while on a walking tour, at the home of a man named Rice. This man seemed to be inhospitable both because of the rudeness of his household, and his own brusk manner, but underneath this he does have a genuine sense for the obligations of a host. His behavior is contrasted with that of the man Thoreau meets shortly after leaving the Rice household. This other man is really rude and uncivil; the two are carefully balanced as contrasts. In the final text of the Rice episode, Thoreau carefully builds up the apparent hostility of the household, leading up to the point where

> At length Rice himself came in, for it was now dark, with an ox-whip in his hand, breathing hard, and he too soon settled down into his seat not far from me, as if, now his day's work was done, he had no farther to travel, but only to digest his supper at his leisure.[7]

In the manuscript version, Thoreau wrote that

> At length Rice himself came in, with an oxwhip in his hand, and breathing hard, and going to a corner drank some kind of liquor.[8]

The second change in Thoreau's text occurs just before Thoreau is ready to retire, when he asks for a lamp. The final version says that

> as he lighted the lamp I detected a gleam of true hospitality and ancient civility, a beam of pure and even gentle humanity, from his bleared and moist eyes. It was a look more intimate with me and more explanatory, than any words of his could have been.[9]

In the earlier manuscript, this passage had read:

> and as he lighted the lamp and handed [it to me] I could see a gleam of true hospitality and ancient civility—a beam of pure and even gentle humanity, from his bleared and moist eyes, for the effect of the liquor had in some measure worked off.[10]

What Thoreau has done here is to eliminate all references to Rice's drinking. He wished to portray the man as hospitable by nature despite the incredibly rude treatment he gave his guest in the social niceties of conversation. The early version attributes some of his rough exterior to alcohol, for Thoreau attributes the "gleam of hospitality" to a more sober host. These references are dropped be-

---

[7] *A Week*, p. 216.
[8] HM 956.
[9] *A Week*, p. 218.
[10] HM 956.

cause it would have weakened the point of the story if
Rice had simply been in a particularly bad mood during
the talk. His rudeness had to be constant if Thoreau, as
he says, was not to "quarrel with nature." What measure
of graciousness Rice possessed is all the more effective
because, in the final version, he is completely in control
of himself. Thoreau thus makes a man a little better than
he was, that he might more gracefully bear the praise
accorded him.

All of these examples point in the direction of change
from the merely amusing to the morally instructive, from
the specifically individual and particular to those particu-
lars best made generally representative and symbolic, and
from the strongly negative tone or fact to the more mod-
erate or positive attitude. No one character in *A Week* is
given much space; even Thoreau himself is less biographi-
cally alive than in *Walden*. A great many people are
mentioned—people met on this trip, people Thoreau had
met on earlier excursions, and historical personages memo-
rialized as the worthies of the local scene through which
they were passing.

Together, these personages form an important part of
the book—they serve always to inhabit the landscape,
taking their place in a tradition which is created partially
by memories of men like John Stark, whom Thoreau uses
to build the sense of a high past which the people of his
time must emulate. The records of the heroes are there if
one looks for them; many of these men, Thoreau tells us,
were "ploughing when the news of the massacre at Lexington arrived, and straightway left their plows in the
furrow, and repaired to the scene of action . . . Generally
speaking, the land is now, at any rate, very barren of
men, and we doubt if there are as many hundreds as we
read of."[11]

The trip along these two New England rivers is, then,

[11] *A Week*, pp. 270–271.

in no sense a movement away from civilization, though it is certainly a move away from habit and the familiarity that can lead to staleness. It is, among other things, the measure of the difference between this book and *Walden* that Thoreau's second book takes us so deeply into the life of Nature that we have left the village far behind—though physically it was never so far away. *A Week*, on the other hand, takes us from Concord only to take us to a long series of towns; the trip is an actual and imaginative pageant of the relationships between one man's mind and the New England both of, and before his time, and this New England is inhabited by the memories of generosity and courage and high deeds. The conception of character is idealistic; the encounters are usually with figures about whom we learn nothing but good; and the simplicity of this as a psychological view is more than balanced by the fact that heroes, including those of Massachusetts and New Hampshire towns, may be excused from our faults in exchange for their willingness to stand up like monuments on a hilltop, so that we may measure our height against them.

JOSEPH J. MOLDENHAUER

*Walden: The Strategy of Paradox**

I fear chiefly lest my expression may not be *extra-vagant* enough, may not wander far enough beyond the narrow limits of my daily experience, so as to be adequate to the truth of which I have been convinced. *Extra-vagance!* it depends on how you are yarded . . . I desire to speak somewhere *without* bounds; like a man in a waking moment, to men in their waking moments; for I am convinced that I cannot exaggerate enough even to lay the foundation of a true expression.[1]

1.

The idiosyncrasies of Thoreau's personality and opinions are so absorbing that "paradox" has always been a key term in Thoreau scholarship. Critic of government and relentless reporter of tortoises, idealistic philosopher and statistician of tree rings, Transcendental friend who calls for "pure hate" to underprop his love,[2] Thoreau invites description as a paradoxical, enigmatic, or even perverse man. As Joseph Wood Krutch maintains, "to unite without incongruity things ordinarily thought of as incongruous *is* the phenomenon called Thoreau."[3] In *Walden* this tendency toward the resolved contradiction

* Reprinted with permission from the *Graduate Journal* (Fall, 1963).
[1] Henry David Thoreau, *The Writings of Henry David Thoreau*, Walden Edition, 20 vols. (Boston, 1906), II, 357.
[2] *Ibid.*, I, 305.
[3] Joseph Wood Krutch, *Henry David Thoreau* (New York, 1948), p. 286.

may be observed in full flower. Here Thoreau talks only of himself yet "brag[s] for humanity." Self-isolated in a spot as remote, he says, as Cassiopeia's Chair, he strolls to the village "every day or two." Renouncing materialism for a poetic and mystic life, he proudly reports his own material efficiency, even documenting his "economy" with balance sheets. Having bewailed the limitations of science and technology, he painstakingly measures the depth of the pond and counts the bubbles in its ice.

Verbal paradox is to my mind the dominant stylistic feature of *Walden*. The persistent intellectual movement through incongruities, antitheses, and contradictions is strikingly reminiscent of the seventeenth-century writers, including Donne and Sir Thomas Browne, who influenced this later metaphysical. Thoreau's paradoxical assertion— for instance, "Much is published, but little printed"—seems self-contradictory or opposed to reason. As a poetic device it has intimate connections with metaphor, because it remains an absurdity, a nonsense, only so long as the terms are taken at their discursive values. The stumbling block disappears, however, as soon as the reader perceives that Thoreau has shifted a meaning, has made a metaphor or a play on words. The pun, that highly compressed form of analogy in which two logically disparate meanings are forced to share the same phonemic unit, lends itself admirably to Thoreau's purposes: to dramatize his statement by giving it the general *appearance* of a contradiction. The special sense of the understood or resolved paradox results from holding a casual and expected meaning to the side and somewhat out of focus.

The user of paradox thus defines or asserts by indirection, frustrating conventional expectations about language. Thoreau's contemporary, Horace Bushnell, affirmed its usefulness in this scholastic pronouncement: "We never come so near to a truly well rounded view of any truth, as when it is offered paradoxically; that is, under contradictions; that is, when under two or more dictions, which, when taken as dictions, are contrary to one another."[4] In *Walden,* where Thoreau wants to communicate very unconventional truths, this rhetorical device affords him great precision as well as polemical effectiveness.

As one might almost expect, Thoreau deprecated this source of stylistic power. When he set down in the *Journal* a list of his "faults," the first was "Paradoxes,—saying just the opposite,—a style which may be imitated."[5] On another occasion he complained that "My companion tempts me to certain licenses of speech. . . . He asks for a paradox, an eccentric statement, and too often I give it to him."[6] At the outset of Thoreau's literary career, Emerson criticised the *"mannerism"* of "A Winter Walk," objecting particularly to the oxymorons: "for example, to call a cold place sultry, a solitude public, a wilderness *domestic.*"[7] But in spite of these warnings and hesitations (which are echoed, incidentally, in the reservations of some of his most sympathetic later critics), Thoreau did not abandon his paradoxical style. His ironic sensibility embraced it and his seventeenth-century reading revealed its enormous resources. Even Archbishop Whately, the author of his college text in rhetoric, could reluctantly acknowledge its advantages. Thoreau wisely followed the crooked bent of his genius and employed a rhetoric suitable for his needs.

These needs were in part dictated by the nature of Transcendental thinking, with its emphasis upon the perception of a spiritual reality behind the surfaces of things. Nature is an expression of the divine mind; its phenomena, when rightly seen, reveal moral truths. By means of proper

---

[4] Horace Bushnell, *God in Christ: Three Discourses, . . . with a Preliminary Dissertation on Language* (Hartford, 1849), p. 55: cited in Charles Feidelson, Jr., *Symbolism and American Literature* (Chicago, 1953), p. 156.

[5] Thoreau, *The Writings . . . ,* XIII, 7 n.

[6] *Ibid.,* XII, 165.

[7] Walter Harding and Carl Bode, eds., *The Correspondence of Henry David Thoreau* (New York, 1958), p. 137: RWE to HDT, Sept. 18, 1843.

perception, said Emerson, "man has access to the entire \
mind of the Creator," and "is himself the creator" of his
own world.[8] Idealism is the Transcendentalist's necessary
premise: it assures him that things conform to thoughts.
By way of demonstration, Emerson tells his uninitiated
reader to look through his legs at an inverted landscape. √
The pure, healthy, and self-reliant man, whose mind is in
harmony with the Over-soul, continually discerns the
miraculous in the common. But for the timid or degraded
man, whose eyes are clouded by convention, nature will
appear a "ruin or . . . blank." Thoreau was sufficiently √
tough-minded to resist the systematic allegorizing of
nature which Emersonian theory implied; and he placed
far greater emphasis than Emerson upon the "shams and
delusions" which hinder men from seeing the natural
facts themselves. But to recognize one's relations with √
nature is for Thoreau the basis of spiritual insight; and
the simplification of life provides the conditions for this
wisdom. Strip away the artificial, Thoreau tells the
"desperate" man, and you will be able to read Nature's
language. Reality, the "secret of things," lurks under
appearances, waiting to be seen.

While Emerson's is a strategy of revelation or illumina-
tion, Thoreau's is a practical strategy of persuasion.
Describing his conversations with the French-Canadian √
woodchopper, Thoreau says he tried to "maneuver" him
"to take the spiritual view."[9] These terms are applicable
generally to the verbal strategies of *Walden*. The problem
Thoreau faced there—to some extent, indeed, in all his
writings—was to create in his audience the "waking
moments" in which they could appreciate "the truth of
which [he had] been convinced." In other words, he tries
to wrench into line with his own the reader's attitudes

[8] Ralph Waldo Emerson, *The Complete Works of Ralph Waldo Emerson*, Centenary Edition, 12 vols. (Boston, 1903), I, 64.
[9] Thoreau, *The Writings* . . . , II, 166.

toward the self, toward society, toward Nature, and toward God. In this effort Thoreau employed a rhetoric of powerful exaggeration and antithesis. Habitually aware of the "common sense," the dulled perception that desperate life produces, he could turn the world of his audience upside down by rhetorical means. He explores new resources of meaning in their "rotten diction" and challenges ingrained habits of thought and action with ennobling alternatives: "Read not the Times," he says in "Life Without Principle." "Read the Eternities."[10] With all the features of his characteristic extravagance—hyperbole, pun, paradox, mock-heroics, loaded questions, and the ironic application of cliché, proverb, and allusion—Thoreau urges new perspectives upon his reader.

2.

Walden is not, of course, merely a sophisticated sermon. It is the story of an experiment; a narrative; a fable. In 1851, while he was wrestling with the book's instructive and factual content, Thoreau wrote, "My facts shall be falsehoods to the common sense. I would so state facts that they shall be significant, shall be myths or mythologic."[11] Even the most hortatory sections of the book are grounded in this "mythology" or significant fiction. I hope to demonstrate that paradox is apposite to the literary design of *Walden*: its themes, symbols, characters, and plot.

As has been pointed out by a number of literary theorists, we can to some extent isolate "a fictional hero with a fictional audience" in any literary work.[12] Clearly the

---

[10] *Ibid.*, IV, 475.

[11] *Ibid.*, IX, 99.

[12] Northrop Frye, *Anatomy of Criticism* (Princeton, N. J., 1957), p. 53. See also W. K. Wimsatt, Jr., *The Verbal Icon* (Lexington, Ky., 1954), p. xv; John Crowe Ransom, *The World's Body* (New York, 1938), p. 247ff; René Wellek, "Closing Statement," in Thomas A. Sebeok, ed., *Style in Language* (New York, 1960), p. 414.

"I" of *Walden*, Thoreau as its narrator and hero, is a delib- ⟍
erately created verbal personality, not to be confused in
critical analysis with Concord's pencil-maker. This narrator
is a man of various moods and self-conscious poses. He is
by turns a severe moralist, a genial companion, a bemused
"hermit," and a whimsical trickster who can regard the
experiment as a sly joke on solid citizens. The mellowest
of all his moods is the one we find in "Baker Farm," "Brute
Neighbors," and "House-Warming," when he pokes fun at
his own zeal as an idealist and reformer. In all these roles ⟍
he conveys a sense of his uniqueness, the separateness of ⟍
his vision from that of his townsmen.

The "fictional audience" of *Walden* likewise requires
attention. In defining it I take a hint from Kenneth Burke,
who in "Antony in Behalf of the Play" discriminates between the play-mob and the spectator-mob as audiences
for the oratory in *Julius Caesar*. Without much danger of
critical high-handedness, we can distinguish in *Walden* a
range of response *within* the dramatic context from a
much broader external response. The reader in part projects himself into the role of a hypothetical "listener,"
whom the narrator addresses directly; and in part he
stands at a remove, overhearing this address. Artistically,
we are "beside ourselves in a sane sense,"[13] both spectators who respond to *Walden* as an aesthetic entity and
projected participants in the verbal action. As spectators,
or what I will call "readers," we are sympathetic toward
the witty and engaging narrator. As participants, or what
I call "listeners" or "audience," we must imagine ourselves
committed to the prejudices and shortsightedness which
the narrator reproves. The rhetoric of *Walden*, reflecting
in some measure the lecture origins of the early drafts,
assumes an initially hostile audience. Thoreau sets up this
role for us. In the first third of "Economy" he characterizes
a mixed group of silent listeners who are suspicious of the

[13] Thoreau, *The Writings* . . . , II, 149.

speaking voice. He would address "poor students," "the mass of men who are discontented," and "that seemingly wealthy, but most terribly impoverished class of all, who have accumulated dross." In addition Thoreau creates vocal antagonists, hecklers who embrace their "mean and sneaking lives." "A certain class of unbelievers," "some inveterate cavillers," "housewives . . . and elderly people," "the hard-featured farmer," " a factory-owner"—such stylized characters complain of Thoreau's unphilanthropic behavior, his agricultural methods, his conclusions about the pond's depth, his manner of making bread, and the cleanliness of his bed linen. Their inquiries tend to be "impertinent" to the lower as well as the higher aspects of the experiment. Their function is to localize and articulate objections which might be raised by the listeners. Thoreau answers these animadversions, implicit and explicit, with every form of irony: puns, paradoxes, perverse proverbs, facetious solemnity, and outright ridicule. The rhetoric of *Walden* is thus determined by the dramatic relationship between the narrator and his audience.

In the satirical and hortatory passages particularly, we are conscious of our aesthetic bifurcation. As listeners, we are incredulous, puzzled, shocked, capable of being persuaded. As readers we are delighted by the rhetorical devastation of the listeners' premises. The instructive values of *Walden* are certainly genuine for us, but they are contained within its artistic values. Even a reader who brought to the book a well developed set of prejudices and hostilities would be encouraged by the force of Thoreau's satirical casuistry to adopt the role of a spectator. For the fictional audience or listener, *Walden* is, in E. B. White's admirable phrase, "an invitation to life's dance."[14] The sympathetic reader dances with Thoreau from the start.

Thoreau's paradoxes are also congenial to the plot and themes of *Walden*. The term "comedy," which I will apply

---

[14] E. B. White, "Walden—1954," *Yale Review*, XLIV (1954), 13.

to its narrative movement, need not be rejected as a misnomer on generic grounds. Using the categories of Professor Northrop Frye, we can consider comedy one of the four "mythoi" or recurrent patterns of plot development which may appear in any genre. The "mythos of spring" or comic plot is characterized by a rising movement, "from a society controlled by habit, ritual bondage, arbitrary law and the older characters to a society controlled by youth and pragmatic freedom . . . a movement from illusion to reality."[15] This generalization of Frye's may call to mind a passage in "Conclusion" where Thoreau proclaims the joys of the "awakened" man: "new, universal, and more liberal laws will begin to establish themselves around and within him; or the old laws be expanded, and interpreted in his favor in a more liberal sense, and he will live with the license of a higher order of beings." On the human level, *Walden's* narrator performs this ascent. On the level of Nature, the green life of spring and summer must rise from old winter's bondage, repeating the hero's own movement and prefiguring the spiritual transformation of his audience, "man in the larva state."

Following a traditional comic pattern, Thoreau represents in *Walden* two worlds: the narrator's private paradise and the social wasteland he has abandoned. Each of these polar worlds, the desirable and the objectionable, has its basic character type and body of symbols. The narrator is the *Eiron*, the virtuous or witty character whose actions are directed toward the establishment of an ideal order. The listeners and hecklers, who take for granted "what are deemed 'the most sacred laws of society,' "[16] serve as the *Alazon* or impostor. This comic type is a braggart, misanthrope, or other mean-spirited figure, usually an older man, who resists the hero's efforts to establish harmony but who is often welcomed into the ideal order when the

[15] Frye, p. 169.
[16] Thoreau, *The Writings* . . . , II, 355.

hero succeeds. The narrator of *Walden,* both virtuous and witty, withdraws from a society of "skin-flint[s]" to a greenwood world at the pond. His pastoral sanctuary is represented in images of moisture, freedom, health, the waking state, fertility, and birth. The society he has rejected is described in images of dust, imprisonment, disease, blindness, lethargy, and death. Upon these symbolic materials Thoreau builds many of his paradoxes. In his verbal attacks upon the old society, whose "idle and musty virtues" he finds as ridiculous as its vices, the narrator assumes an ironic or denunciatory pose. When he records and praises his simple *vita nuova,* that is, in the idyllic passages, his tone becomes meditative or ecstatic.

3.

But, after all, it is to the dusty world or wasteland that *Walden's* fictional audience belongs. Despite their dissatisfactions, they are committed to this life and its values, and are thus effectively blind to the practical as well as the spiritual advantages of the experiment. The narrator, far from being a misanthropic skulker, wishes to communicate his experience of a more harmonious and noble life. His language serves this end: the first rhetorical function of paradox is to make the listener entertain a crucial doubt. Does he value houses? Thoreau calls them prisons, almshouses, coffins, and family tombs. Farming? It is digging one's own grave. Equipment and livestock? Herds are the keepers of men, not men of herds; and men are "the tools of their tools." Traditional knowledge and a Harvard education? Thoreau describes them as impediments to wisdom. Financial security, or "something [laid up] against a sick day," is the cause of sickness in the man who works for it. Fine and fashionable clothing is a form of decoration more barbaric than tattooing, which is only "skin-deep." The landlord's sumptuous furnishings are really "traps" which hold the holder captive. The railroad, marvel of the industrial age, is a means of transportation ultimately slower than going afoot. Religion, Thoreau tells his pious audience, is a "cursing of God" and distrust of themselves. "Good business," the bulwark of their culture, is the quickest way to the devil. In short, says Thoreau, "The greater part of what my neighbors call good I believe in my soul to be bad, and if I repent of anything, it is very likely to be my good behavior. What demon possessed me that I behaved so well?" These paradoxes, often executed with brilliant humor, jostle and tumble the listener's perspective. To be sure, the narrator is a self-acknowledged eccentric—but he is not a lunatic. Thoreau makes sense in his own terms, and the fictive audience no longer can in theirs.

At the same time as he makes nonsense and carnage of the listener's vocabulary with satirical paradoxes, Thoreau appropriates some of its key terms to describe the special values of the experiment. For example, though he despises commerce he would conduct a profitable trade with the Celestial Empire. In this second body of rhetorical devices Thoreau again exploits polarities of symbol and idea, and not without some irony. But these paradoxes differ significantly in their function from the satirical ones. They attach to the Transcendentalist's world, to nature and simplicity, the deep connotations of value which "appearances" evoke for the desperate man. Thoreau astounds and disarms the audience when he calls his experiment a "business," and renders his accounts to the half- and quarter-penny. By means of this appropriately inappropriate language he announces the incompatibility of his "living" and his neighbor's, and simultaneously suggests interesting resemblances. His "trade," like the businessman's, requires risks, demands perseverance, and holds out the lure of rewards. The statistical passages of "Economy" and "The Bean-Field" are ambiguous. On the one hand, they illustrate the narrator's ability to beat the thrifty Yankee at his own

game; on the other they parody the Yankee's obsession
with finance. Thoreau's argument that one is successful in
proportion as he reduces his worldly needs is likewise
paradoxical, a queer analogue to the commercial theory of
increasing profits by lowering costs. He reinforces this
unconventional economic principle by declaring that the
simple life is to be carefully cultivated and jealously pre-
served: "Give me the poverty that enjoys true wealth."
Similarly he contrasts the rich harvest which a poet reaps
from a farm with the *relatively* worthless cash crop, and
is eager to acquire the Hollowell place before its owner
destroys it with "improvements." I would also include in
this category of paradoxes Thoreau's constant reference to
fish, berries, and other "common" natural objects in the
language of coins, precious gems, and rare metals; his
praise of the humble simpleton as an exalted sage; his
assertion that the woods and ponds are religious sanctu-
aries; and his description of his labors as pastimes and his
solitude as companionable. Some related statements carry
overtones of the New Testament: "Not till we are lost, in
other words, not till we have lost the world, do we begin
to find ourselves." "Walden was dead and is alive again."
All these apparent contradictions emphasize the trium-
phant subjectivism of *Walden,* Thoreau's running declaration that "The universe constantly and obediently answers
to our conceptions."[17] The highest and most sincere conception yields the noblest life.

By nature a dialectical instrument, the paradox is thus
stylistically integral to this severely dialectical work. Generally speaking, the two large groups of paradoxes reflect
the comic structure of *Walden* and its two major themes:
the futility of the desperate life and the marvellousness
of enlightened simplicity. With the paradoxes of the first
or satirical group, Thoreau declares that his listener's
goods are evils, his freedom slavery, and his life a death.

[17] *Ibid.,* II, 108.

Those of the second group, corresponding rhetorically to what Sherman Paul calls *Walden's* metamorphoses, proclaim that the values of the natural and transcendental life arise from what the listener would deprecate as valueless. In these paradoxes, the beautiful is contained in the ugly, the truly precious in the seemingly trivial, and the springs of life in the apparently dead.

As *Walden* progresses the proportion of the first to the second kind gradually changes. The rhetoric of the early chapters is very largely one of trenchant denunciation, directed against the desperate life. That of the later chapters is predominantly serene, playful, and rapturous. Thoreau creates the impression of a growing concord between himself and his audience by allowing the caustic ironies and repudiations of "Economy" to shift by degrees to the affirmations of "Spring" and "Conclusion." Thoreau the outsider becomes Thoreau the magnanimous insider, around whom reasonable men and those who love life may gather. Rhetorically and thematically, as the book proceeds, the attack becomes the dance.

4.

To return from structural to textural considerations, I should like at this point to examine in detail one of the many passages in *Walden* controlled by verbal paradox. The following, from "Where I Lived and What I Lived For," demonstrates, I believe, Thoreau's intellectual virtuosity and his control of humor for polemical ends:

> We do not ride on the railroad; it rides upon us. Did you ever think what those sleepers are that underlie the railroad? Each one is a man, an Irishman, or a Yankee man. The rails are laid on them, and they are covered with sand, and the cars run smoothly over them. They are sound sleepers, I assure you. And every few years a new lot is laid down and run over; so that, if some have the pleasure of riding on a rail, others have the misfortune to

be ridden upon. And when they run over a man that is walking in his sleep, a supernumerary sleeper in the wrong position, and wake him up, they suddenly stop the cars, and make a hue and cry about it, as if this were an exception. I am glad to know that it takes a gang of men for every five miles to keep the sleepers down and level in their beds . . . for this is a sign that they may sometime get up again.

The punning word "sleepers," referring simultaneously to the railroad ties and to the benighted laborers who lay them, supports the paradox "We do not ride on the railroad; it rides upon us." The repetitions in the short third sentence—"man . . . Irishman . . . Yankee man"—vigorously relate the miserable workers to the more fortunate riders of the cars; they are all in the human family. The train rides on mankind in the sense that a *man* would degrade his life in the railroad enterprise, working on the tracks all day for a pittance. His life is a form of death; metaphorically he has been buried, like the wooden sleepers which he himself has covered with sand. He may stay "buried" or "asleep" for many years; perhaps as long as the wooden ties, the "sound sleepers," remain solid and unrotted. When Thoreau remarks, "if some have the pleasure of riding on a rail, others have the misfortune to be ridden upon," he ironically suggests a brutal insouciance on the part of those wealthy enough to travel over an extension of the track, laid by new workers. But in terms of the opening statement, the travelers share the misfortune of being ridden upon; they are to an extent themselves "sleepers" or unenlightened men. The occasional sleepwalker struck by the train is very likely an exhausted laborer, walking on the track in the mental and moral stupor typical of his way of life. Thoreau calls him a "supernumerary sleeper," equating once more the literal block of wood with the wooden man who places it. But "in the wrong position" involves a new paradox: instead of walking stupidly and sleepily on the track—preserving a merely physical uprightness—he should perhaps have wholly abandoned himself to his futile labor and lain down with the ties. Nevertheless, his calamity excites a "hue and cry." In terms of the railroad's "economy" he should have been at the same time a sleeper and not a sleeper. To be struck and run over by the train, or literally to assume the position of the wooden sleepers in man's last and permanent sleep, is to be withdrawn from the fruitless life of track-laying, or to be "awakened." For if the laborer's life is *figuratively* a death and a sleep, his *actual* death, the end of that existence, would be a birth or a waking. Finally, Thoreau sees in the restlessness of the ties, their tendency to shift in the roadbed, an intimation that the very men who keep the ties down and level may themselves awaken to the dawn of their day, and rise.

5.

Time limitations prevent me from extending my analysis to the paradoxes which control individual chapters, such as "Higher Laws," and fully developed arguments such as the discussion of philanthropy in the first chapter. Nor can I examine at length the juxtaposed rhythms of rise and fall, ascent and descent, primitivism and transcendence which pervade the imagery and action of the book. In this last connection, however, we might briefly note that the Transcendental distinction between what *"is"* and what *"appears* to be" is reflected in the recurrent contrasting of surface and subsurface phenomena. When the narrator chases the diving loon, or fishes for pouts at night, he acts out his pursuit of higher truth. Common sense will provide only superficial catches; the earnest truth-seeker, the "hunter and fisher of men," must search beneath appearances and within himself. The pond in its most consistent symbolic role is the self, the beholder's own profound nature. Here, as elsewhere, Thoreau ascends by descending: on dark nights his fishing line is lost in the black water below, and his line of thought wanders in "vast and cosmogonal themes in other spheres." The bite of the pout links him to Nature again, and as the fish comes wriggling upward, the mind pins down an intuition to a perceived fact. "Thus I caught two fishes as it were with one hook." Legislators prescribe the number of fishhooks to be permitted at Walden, "but they know nothing about the hook of hooks with which to angle for the pond itself, impaling the legislature for a bait." Thoreau, however, has mastered this fishing lore; he sacrifices social institutions in the quest for himself, for reality. In a similar paradox, Thoreau admits that "Snipes and woodcocks . . . may afford rare sport; but I trust it would be nobler game to shoot one's self."

"Conclusion," which is richer in paradoxes than any other chapter, announces the grand prospects of the awakened life: "In proportion as [a man] simplifies his life, the laws of the universe will appear less complex, and solitude will not be solitude, nor poverty poverty, nor weakness weakness." The climactic passages of the chapter are two dramatized paradoxes, fables of metamorphosis. In the first, the timeless artist of Kouroo, like the liberated human spirit Thoreau is celebrating, creates a new and glorious world around himself. The second fable, more humble in its materials but not less marvelous in its import, is the anecdote of a bug which emerges from "society's most trivial and handselled furniture," to enjoy a beautiful and winged life after a long death. With a series of symbolic and paradoxical aphorisms—"Only that day dawns to which we are awake. . . . The sun is but a morning star"—the book concludes.

WALTER HARDING

The Last Days of
Henry Thoreau*

Although Henry David Thoreau was
plagued with recurring attacks of active tuberculosis from
his college days onward, we can date the beginning of
his final illness with precision—December 3, 1860. Thoreau
spent the afternoon on Fair Haven Hill studying the
growth of hickories and oaks. It was a raw, bleak day and
he caught cold. When, against doctor's advice, he insisted
on fulfilling a lecture engagement in Waterbury, Connec-
ticut, on the 11th, the strain of the journey was too much
for him. The cold rapidly worsened into bronchitis, which
in turn reopened the old tubercular lesions in his lungs.
He was confined to his house for the rest of the winter.

With the coming of spring doctors urged him to try a
drier climate and he made a futile two-month journey to
Minnesota and back with Horace Mann, Jr., the son of
the famed educator. In the early fall of 1861 he seemed
briefly to recover somewhat, but within a few weeks there
was a relapse. By late November he was confined to the
house once more. By mid-December he had failed so much
that he could no longer hold a pen and was forced to dic-
tate all his writing to his sister Sophia. On the 19th of
December, 1861, Sophia wrote Daniel Ricketson, Thoreau's
New Bedford friend:

* Reprinted with permission from *American Heritage*, XIV (December,
1962), 106–112.

31

The air and exercise which he [Thoreau] enjoyed during the fine autumn days, was a benefit to him—he seemed stronger—had a good appetite, and was able to attend somewhat to his writing; but since the cold weather has come his cough has increased and he is able to go out but seldom. Just now he is suffering from an attack of pleurisy which confines him wholly to the house.

His spirits do not fail him, he continues in his usual serene mood, which is very pleasant for his friends as well as himself.

When Bronson Alcott called on New Year's Day, 1862, bringing cider and apples, he found Thoreau failing and feeble, but talkative and interested in books and men. They discussed Pliny, Evelyn, and the rural authors. When Alcott mentioned the war, Thoreau spoke impatiently of "the temporizing policy" of the government and blamed "the people too for their indifference to the true issues of national honor and justice." But despite Thoreau's brave talk, Alcott thought it obvious that his days were numbered, that as Alcott phrased it—"The spring's summons must come for him soon to partake of 'Syrian peace, Immortal leisure.' "

A week later Daniel Ricketson wrote, inviting Thoreau to visit him in New Bedford. But Alcott, at Sophia Thoreau's request, replied:

He grows feebler day by day, and is evidently failing and fading from our sight. He gets some sleep, has a pretty good appetite, reads at intervals, takes notes of his readings, and likes to see his friends, conversing, however, with difficulty, as his voice partakes of his general debility.

His old Worcester friends, H. G. O. Blake and Theo Brown, skated down the river from Framingham to visit Thoreau in mid-January—a journey they repeated several times in the succeeding months. Brown said of the visit:

We found him pretty low, but well enough to be up in his chair. He seemed glad to see us; said we had not come much too soon. . . . There was a beautiful snowstorm going on the while which I fancy inspired him, and his talk was up to the best I ever heard from him,—the same depth of earnestness and the same infinite depth of fun going on at the same time.

I wish I could recall some of the things he said. I do remember some few answers he made to questions from Blake. Blake asked him how the future seemed to him. "Just as uninteresting as ever," was his characteristic answer. A little while after he said, "You have been skating on this river; perhaps I am going to skate on some other." And again, "Perhaps I am going up country. . . ." He seemed to be in an exalted state of mind for a long time before his death. He said it was just as good to be sick as to be well,—just as good to have a poor time as a good time.

About this same time Thoreau received a letter from a stranger, Myron Benton, a young poet from Leedsville, New York, saying that news of Thoreau's illness had affected him as if it were that of a personal friend whom he had known a long time. He said he had read and reread Thoreau's books with ever fresh delight and asked what progress he had made on a work in "some way connected with history,"—which Emerson had told him about in a short interview two years before in Poughkeepsie. (It was probably Thoreau's never-completed "Atlas of Concord" to which Emerson had referred.)

It was mid-March before Thoreau was able to answer Benton's letter, and then, dictating to his sister, he said:

I have intended to answer before I died, however briefly. I am encouraged to know, that, so far as you are concerned, I have not written my books in vain. . . . You ask particularly after my health. I *suppose* that I have not many months to live; but, of course, I know nothing about it. I may add that I am enjoying existence as much as ever, and regret nothing.

As ill as he was, Thoreau nevertheless continued his literary work. Early in February a request came from James T. Fields for Thoreau to submit some of his writings to the *Atlantic Monthly*. Ticknor & Fields, the publishers of *Walden*, had purchased the *Atlantic* in 1859 from Phillips, Sampson & Co. In June, 1861, Fields had taken over its editorial direction. Since James Russell Lowell, who had arbitrarily censored one of Thoreau's essays earlier, now no longer had any connection with the magazine, Thoreau was happy to accede to Fields' request. But, remembering his unpleasant experience with Lowell, he wrote Fields: "Of course, I should expect that no sentiment or sentence be altered or omitted without my consent" and then carefully asked how much Fields would be willing to pay.

Thoreau apparently received a satisfactory answer and on February 20th submitted a manuscript based on his lecture on "Autumnal Tints." Fields accepted it and asked for another essay more appropriate to the spring season. He also suggested that he would be interested in bringing *Walden* back into print. (It had been out-of-print for several years.) Thoreau immediately replied that he would soon send along another essay and that not only would he be very happy to see *Walden* back in print, but that he had 146 bound copies and 450 unbound copies of his first book, *A Week*, in his attic—an obvious hint to Fields that he would like to see the earlier book republished too.

On February 26th Thoreau submitted an essay which he had entitled "The Higher Law." It was derived from a lecture that he had been delivering for nearly a decade, sometimes under the title of "Getting a Living" and sometimes as "What Shall It Profit [a man if he gain the whole world but lose his own soul]?" After paying Thoreau one hundred dollars for the essay, Fields, perhaps fearing that it might be confused with the chapter entitled "Higher Laws" in *Walden*, complained that he did not like the title. They soon agreed on a new title—"Life without Principle"—but the essay itself was not published in the *Atlantic* until October of 1863. They also agreed to the reprinting of *Walden* in a new edition of 250 copies (actually 280 were printed just a few weeks after Thoreau's death) and Thoreau's request that the subtitle "or Life in the Woods" be dropped was followed.

On March 11th Thoreau returned the proofs of "Autumnal Tints" (it was published in the October, 1862, *Atlantic*) and submitted his essay on "Walking." It was immediately accepted and published in the June, 1862, *Atlantic*. On April 2nd Thoreau submitted "Wild Apples," which was accepted and then published in November, 1862, and asked Fields if he had come to any decision about republishing *A Week*. On the 12th Fields purchased all the unsold copies—bound and unbound—of the book and two months later reissued them with a new title page as a second edition. (Oddly enough he neglected to remove the advertisement at the rear announcing that *Walden* would "soon be published.")

It was in April that Bronson Alcott's anonymous tribute to Thoreau appeared in the *Atlantic* under the title "The Forester," and saying, in part:

> I had never thought of knowing a man so thoroughly of the country as this friend of mine, and so purely a son of nature. . . . He has come nearer the antique spirit than any of our native poets, and touched the fields and groves and streams of his native town with a classic interest that shall not fade. . . . One shall not meet with thoughts invigorating like his often: coming so scented of mountain and field breezes and rippling springs, so like a luxuriant clod from under forest-leaves, moist and mossy with earth-spirits. . . .
>
> He seems one with things, of nature's essence and core, knit of strong timbers, most like a wood and its inhabitants. . . .
>
> I know of nothing more creditable to his greatness than the thoughtful regard, approaching to reverence, by which he has held for many years some of the best persons of his time, living at a distance, and wont to make their annual pilgrimage, usually on foot, to the master,—a devotion

very rare in these times of personal indifference, if not of confessed unbelief in persons and ideas.

Although Thoreau is not mentioned directly by name in the essay, the many references to Walden Pond and to a book on the rivers made its subject perfectly obvious to his friends and acquaintances. That knowledge of its subject was widespread is indicated from a contemporary newspaper comment:

> "The Forrester" [sic] is a touching, interpretative and beautiful tribute to the genius of Henry D. Thoreau, of Concord,—a man now failing, we fear, under the insidious disease peculiar to New England, but whose works prove him to be the subtlest of all observers of New England scenery. Few men have ever observed nature so exactly, ever entered so thoroughly into the interior life which her outward form partly expresses and partly conceals to ordinary minds, as this brave and poetic naturalist; and the lyric extravagance which marks some of the phrases of the poet-philosopher who here celebrates his virtues will be readily pardoned by criticism as they are excusable on the ground of friendship and sympathy.

Daniel Ricketson, reminded of Thoreau by the appearance of Alcott's "Forester" and word of the forthcoming republication of *Walden*, started a weekly series of letters to cheer his old friend by noting the progress of the spring. On March 23rd he wrote of the arrival of the robin, the bluebird, the song sparrow, and the cowbird and on the 30th of the coming of the purple finch and some of the warblers. In the latter letter he added the quaint suggestion that Thoreau's health might improve if he would only move where he could breathe in the fragrance of the pines. He even suggested that Thoreau move to a particular pine grove in Plymouth, some seventy miles south of Concord.

On the 6th of April Sophia Thoreau replied to Ricketson, reporting of her brother:

> Now the embodiment of weakness; still, he enjoys seeing his friends, and every bright hour he devotes to his manu-

scripts which he is preparing for publication. For many weeks he has spoken only in a faint whisper. Henry accepts this dispensation with such childlike trust and is so happy that I feel as if he were being translated rather than dying in the ordinary way of most mortals.

On the 13th, Ricketson wrote again, saying:

> Truly you have not lived in vain—your works, and above all your brave and truthful life, will become a precious treasure to those whose happiness it has been to have known you, and who will continue to uphold though with feebler hands the fresh and instructive philosophy you have taught them.

Thoreau, though, was disturbed that Ricketson did not come to Concord to see him. When he learned that it was because Ricketson feared his "own ability to endure the strain of his nerves at seeing Thoreau's then emaciated appearance, and the leave-taking that would follow," Thoreau whispered to his sister, "Now Ricketson ought to come and see me; it would do him good."

But Thoreau's other friends and neighbors did not shy away. Emerson dropped in frequently to talk of chickadees, the behaviour of the river, the ice on Walden Pond, and the arrival of the spring birds. On March 23rd Sam Staples, who sixteen years before had placed Thoreau in jail, dropped in for a visit. He later told Emerson that he had "never spent an hour with more satisfaction. Never saw a man dying with so much pleasure and peace." He thought Thoreau to be "serene and happy" and lamented that "very few men in Concord really knew him."

Thoreau was pathetically interested in the world of Nature bypassing him that spring. On a cold morning he tried vainly to scrape the frost from the window pane, saying with utter sadness, as he failed, "I cannot even *see* out-doors." He often asked his sister to throw open the doors to the adjacent room so that he could admire her conservatory of potted plants. And learning that young Edward Emerson was planning a trip to the Far West, he urged him to find an Indian who could at last tell the secret of the making of stone arrowheads. When he learned that some boys in the neighborhood had been robbing birds' nests, he requested that they be called into his sick room and "was heard asking them if they knew what a wail of sorrow and anguish their cruelty had sent all over the fields and through the woods."

But Thoreau did not lose his sense of humor. He told Sanborn that whenever his corpulent, chubby-faced aunt came to his chamber door to inquire about his welfare, he thought her to be "the rising full moon." When someone commented how little his hair had grayed, even in his illness, he replied:

> I have never had any trouble in all my life, or only when I was about fourteen; then I felt pretty bad a little while on account of my sins, but no trouble since that I know of. That must be the reason why my hair doesn't turn gray faster. But there is Blake; he is as gray as a rat.

When Grindall Reynolds, the minister of Concord's First Parish Church, called and found him still working on his manuscripts, Thoreau "looked up cheerfully and, with a twinkle in his eye, whispered . . . 'You know it's respectable to leave an estate to one's friends.'"

Less than two weeks before his death, finding it difficult to rouse himself for work, he complained to Channing that he could not see to correct his Allegash paper—the final chapter in *The Maine Woods*—saying, "It is in a knot I cannot untie."

Thoreau realized fully that the end was near. He told Channing that he could never feel warm again, that he had no wish to live except for the sake of his mother and sister, and that, "It is better some things should end." To Bronson Alcott he said, "I shall leave the world without regret." And when Edmund Hosmer told him of seeing a spring robin, Thoreau replied, "Yes! This is a beautiful world; but I shall see a fairer."

He was greatly moved by the attentions of his friends and neighbors. It was said that he "came to feel very differently toward people, and said if he had known he wouldn't have been so offish. He had got into his head before that people didn't mean what they said."

> The devotion of his friends [said his sister Sophia] was most rare and touching; his room was made fragrant by the gift of flowers from young and old; fruit of every kind which the season afforded, and game of all sorts was sent him. It was really pathetic, the way in which the town was moved to minister to his comfort. Total strangers sent grateful messages, remembering the good he had done them. All this attention was fully appreciated and very gratifying to Henry; he would sometimes say, "I should be ashamed to stay in this world after so much had been done for me, I could never repay my friends."

Remembering how much Thoreau had enjoyed their music box when they had first moved to Concord twenty years before, the Hawthornes brought it to his sickroom. Mrs. Alcott sent over some spearmint from her garden to be used as a tonic, saying in a note to Mrs. Thoreau, "I wish I had some delicacy for the dear patient—but we have none of those things usually so grateful and appetising to the sick."

When Thoreau learned that some of the boys of the neighborhood had brought him some game to eat, he asked, "Why did you not invite them in? I want to thank them for so much that they are bringing me," and added, "Well, I declare; I don't believe they are going to let me go after all."

> In his last illness [a child of the neighborhood recalls] it did not occur to us that he would care to see us, but his sister told my mother that he watched us from the window as we passed, and said: "Why don't they come to see me? I love them as if they were my own." After that we went often, and he always made us so welcome that we liked to go. I remember our last meetings with as much pleasure as the old play-days.

When Thoreau heard a wandering street singer playing some old tune of his childhood on a hand organ in the streets outside, tears came to his eyes and he said, "Give him some money! give him some money!"

As long as he could possibly sit up, he insisted on his chair at the family table, and said, "It would not be social to take my meals alone." When he could no longer negotiate the stairs even with assistance, he requested that the little cane bed he had used at Walden be brought down and placed in the front parlor.

> This room did not seem like a sick-room [said his mother]. My son wanted flowers and pictures and books all around here; and he was always so cheerful and wished others to be so while about him.

Sleeplessness often bothered him. He wished his bed were in the form of a shell so that he might curl up in it. At night he asked that the lamp be set on the floor and the furniture arranged so that he could amuse himself watching the fantastic shadows. He refused opiates, telling Channing that " he preferred to endure with a clear mind the worst penalties of suffering, rather than be plunged in a turbid dream of narcotics." Nevertheless when he did sleep he was troubled with strange dreams. "Sleep seemed to hang round my bed in festoons," he told Channing. And he reported a pitiful dream he had "of being a railroad cut, where they were digging through and laying down the rails,—the place being in his lungs."

Nevertheless he kept up his good spirits.

> Henry [said Sophia] was never affected, never reached by [his illness]. I never before saw such a manifestation of the power of spirit over matter. Very often I have heard him tell his visitors that he enjoyed existence as well as ever. He remarked to me that there was as much comfort in perfect disease as in perfect health, the mind always conforming to the condition of the body. The thought of death, he said, could not begin to trouble him. His

thoughts had entertained him all his life and did still. . . .
During his long illness I never heard a murmur escape
him, or the slightest wish expressed to remain with us; his
perfect contentment was truly wonderful. None of his
friends seemed to realize how very ill he was, so full of
life and good cheer did he seem. One friend, as if by way
of consolation, said to him, "Well, Mr. Thoreau, we must
all go." Henry replied, "When I was a very little boy I
learned that I must die, and I set that down, so of course
I am not disappointed now. Death is as near to you as it
is to me."

Some of his more orthodox friends and relatives tried
to prepare him for death in their own way but with little
satisfaction to themselves. When an old friend of the
family asked "how he stood affected toward Christ," he
replied that "a snow-storm was more to him than Christ."
When his aunt asked him if he had made his peace with
God, he answered, "I did not know we had ever quar-
relled, Aunt." Just a few days before the end, Parker
Pillsbury visited the sick room.

He was very weak and low [says Pillsbury]: he saw but
very few more setting suns. He sat pillowed in an easy
chair. Behind him stood his patient, dear, devoted mother,
with her fan in one hand, and phial of ammonia or cologne
in the other, to sustain him in the warm morning. At the
table near him, piled with his papers and other articles
related to them and to him, sat his sister, arranging them,
as I understood, for Ticknor and Fields, who had been to
Concord and bought the copyright.

When I entered Thoreau was looking deathly weak and
pale. I saw my way but for the fewest words. I said, as
I took his hand, "I suppose this is the best you can do
now." He smiled and only nodded, and gasped a faint
assent. "The outworks," I said, "seem almost ready to give
way." Then a smile shone on his pale face, and with an
effort he said, "Yes,—but as long as she cracks she holds"
(a common saying of boys skating).

Then I spoke only once more to him, and cannot remember my exact words. But I think my question was sub-
stantially this: "You seem so near the brink of the dark

river, that I almost wonder how the opposite shore may appear to you." Then he answered, "One world at a time."

On the 4th of May, Alcott and Channing came to call. Alcott came away certain, as he says, that Thoreau had "not many days of his mortality to give us." On the 5th they returned again and found that he was "very weak but suffered nothing and talked in his old pleasant way saying 'it took Nature a long time to do her work but he was most out of the world.'" As they left, Alcott stooped over and kissed him.

> It was affecting [says Channing] to see this venerable man kissing his brow, when the damps and sweat of death lay upon it, even if Henry knew it not. It seemed to me an extreme unction, in which a friend was the best priest.

That evening Thoreau received a last letter from Daniel Ricketson which his sister read to him. Ironically it said:

> I hope this will find you *mending*, and as I hear nothing to the contrary, I trust that it may be so that you are.

A "Mr. B——" had volunteered to sit up the night with him, but Henry wanted his old friend Edmund Hosmer and he was sent for. In the morning when Hosmer was ready to leave, Thoreau called his sister and asked her to give him a copy of one of his books.

At seven o'clock he became restless and asked to be moved. Judge Rockwood Hoar arrived with a bouquet of hyacinths from his garden. Thoreau smelled them and said he liked them. His self-possession did not forsake him. A little after eight he asked to be raised up. The last few weeks of his life he had been working over his Maine Woods papers and his thoughts continued on his writing to the end. The last sentence he spoke contained but two distinct words: "Moose" and "Indian." As his mother, his sister, and his Aunt Louisa watched, his breathing grew fainter and fainter, and without the slightest struggle he died at nine o'clock. Sophia said, "I feel as if something very beautiful had happened—not death."

Plans were immediately started for the funeral. Emerson insisted that it be held in the First Parish Church (Unitarian), though many of his friends protested that Thoreau would have felt such a service inappropriate after his "signing-off" from the church as a young man. And Mrs. Hawthorne complained:

> I ought to be at his funeral for the sake of shewing [sic] my deep respect and value for him to others, though I could better mourn him at home.

Alcott planned the service, patterning the arrangements on those Thoreau himself had made for the John Brown memorial service in Concord three years before. When Alcott called at the home to talk over the plans, Sophia showed him Thoreau's face. He thought Thoreau looked as he had last seen him, but of a tinge of paler hue. Emerson, meanwhile, prepared the eulogy and wrote to various friends, asking them to attend the funeral and inviting them to an early dinner at his home.

The service was held at three on the afternoon of the 9th. Alcott left word with his teachers to dismiss all the children from the schools, and many of them thus attended the funeral. The church was filled. As Louisa May Alcott ironically pointed out to her friend Alfred Whitman, "Though he wasn't made much of while living, he was honored at his death." Hawthorne and his family were there, as were the faithful Blake and Brown from Worcester, James T. Fields and his wife, and Bronson Alcott and his daughters Anna and Louisa May, among others. Daniel Ricketson, too appalled with grief, did not attend.

The casket was in the church vestibule covered with wild flowers. Inside the coffin was a wreath of andromeda —"his favorite flower"—and three mottoes gathered and inscribed by Ellery Channing:

> Hail to thee, O man, who art come from the transitory place to the imperishable.

> Gazed on the Heavens for what he missed on Earth.

I think for to touche also
The world whiche neweth everie daie,
So as I can, so as I maie.

As the bell tolled his forty-four years, the mourners walked in procession to the church. The service opened with selections from the Bible read by the Rev. Grindall Reynolds, minister of the church. A hymn written by Channing and printed for the occasion was sung "plaintively" by the choir.

Emerson read an extensive eulogy. It started off on a negative note:

> He [Thoreau] was a protestant *a outrance*, and few lives contain so many renunciations. He was bred to no profession, he never married; he lived alone; he never went to church; he never voted; he refused to pay a tax to the State; he ate no flesh; he drank no wine; he never knew the use of tobacco; and, though a naturalist, he used neither trap nor gun. . . . It cost him nothing to say No; indeed he found it much easier than to say Yes.

It ended on a more appropriate, more positive note:

> The scale on which his studies proceeded was so large as to require longevity, and we were the less prepared for his sudden disappearance. The country knows not yet, or in the least part, how great a son it has lost. It seems an injury that he should leave in the midst his broken task, which none else can finish,—a kind of indignity to so noble a soul, that it should depart out of Nature before yet he has been really shown to his peers for what he is. But he, at least, is content. His soul was made for the noblest society; he had in a short life exhausted the capabilities of this world; wherever there is knowledge, wherever there is virtue, wherever there is beauty, he will find a home.

Alcott read some passages from Thoreau's writings and the service closed with a prayer by the Rev. Mr. Reynolds.

A new procession was formed to follow the coffin as it was carried by six of his fellow-townsmen to the grave.

If Elbert Hubbard is correct, three fourths of the town's four hundred school children walked in the procession. He was buried in the New Burying Ground, at the foot of Bedford Street. As Emerson turned away from the newly filled grave, he murmured, "He had a beautiful soul, he had a beautiful soul."

Louisa May Alcott afterwards wrote to Sophia Foord (who so many years before had proposed marriage to Thoreau):

> It seemed as if Nature wore her most benignant aspect to welcome her dutiful & loving son to his long sleep in her arms. As we entered the church yard birds were singing, early violets blooming in the grass & the pines singing their softest lullaby, & there between his father & his brother we left him, feeling that though his life seemed too short, it would blossom & bear fruit for us long after he was gone, & that perhaps we should know a closer relationship now than even while he lived.

RAYMOND ADAMS

The Day Thoreau Didn't Die

There are other ways than physically to die. Libraries are cluttered with books whose authors in the sense we want to use the term are dead. Some of them were stillborn writers who never were alive; but some of them lived in their time, then died. Was Thoreau ever in danger of such dying? And when was the day he didn't die?

He was in such danger and he wasn't. We cannot believe that such genius could have gone permanently into oblivion or even been in any real danger of dying. We especially can't, because to us his has been a reputation that has not only been alive as long as we can remember, but that, since the centennial of his birth in 1917, has been flourishing and growing all these forty-five years as the most alive reputation out of his century—not forgetting Whitman, Melville, or Emily Dickinson, those others of the nineteenth century whom the twentieth has delighted to find more alive than when they were alive. Indeed, before 1917, since that great venture in faith entered into by Houghton Mifflin and Company in 1906 by the publication of fourteen volumes of Thoreau's journal (a tremendous risk at the time), the reputation of Thoreau has so steadily advanced on so many fronts that we are unable to imagine a time when it was otherwise. But there was such a time. There was a day when Thoreau did not die. Which day was it? Well, I think it was some day in the late 1870's or early 1880's—not any particular date, of course, but a time when Thoreau's reputation ebbed until he might have died into a nature writer regarded as slightly better than John Burroughs, a social commentator worse than George William Curtis.

What had happened? By the late 1870's Thoreau's reputation had suffered what his early defender Thomas Wentworth Higginson termed "two of the greatest dangers that can beset reputation—a brilliant satirist for a critic, and an injudicious friend for a biographer." These were, of course, James Russell Lowell and Ellery Channing, who, as Higginson pointed out, "brought the eccentricities of Thoreau into undue prominence, and . . . placed too little stress on the vigor, the good sense, the clear perceptions, of the man." Lowell may have been the villain of the piece. Ellery Channing was hardly influential, but Lowell had wide acceptance as a critic. His review essay of *Letters to Various Persons* (a book in which Mr. Emerson's cautious editing had solemnized Thoreau into a proper stoic) was reprinted in 1871 in *My Study Windows* and for a score of years set the tone for Thoreau criticism in America. Channing's *Thoreau, the Poet-Naturalist* two years later was a hodge podge that surely must have been discounted except insofar as it seemed an intimate friend's corroboration of the image Lowell had set up. Channing did contribute a phrase—"the poet-naturalist"—that labeled Thoreau for the next twenty-five years. The effect of a phrasemaker is not to be scorned. No schoolman looked behind Channing's phrase and Lowell's essay, so for a quarter of a century the Thoreau of the textbooks and the school readers was a poet-naturalist with the eccentricities of a Transcendentalist and the unsocial habits of a hermit.

Perhaps the 1880's are equally crucial because early in that decade Mr. Emerson died and the light of reappraisal and praise turned anew on his life pushed Thoreau once again into the background as an Emersonian. Moreover, in the 1880's Mr. Alcott's School of Philosophy brought an Indian summer of Transcendentalism to Concord, confirming in the public mind all the vagaries of the earlier movement and reminding readers again that these qualities had recently been attached to Thoreau by Lowell and ingrained there by Ellery Channing, who, if he couldn't write a book, was thought capable of characterizing his close friend Henry Thoreau. Moreover, Frank Sanborn wrote his dull biography just then and fairly embalmed this partial reputation with misunderstanding.

For these reasons—doubtless for many others—and because of the temper of America's late Victorian time, the label stuck. Thoreau became the poet-naturalist, writing with admittedly unequalled charm about the natural history of Concord much as Gilbert White with another charm had written about Selbourne—and having about as much impact on the thought of the nation during the next forty years as Gilbert White had had on the Industrial Revolution in England during the generation or two after his death. For forty years after 1862 Thoreau was a poet-naturalist, and whatever else he was seemed dead.

That became the persistent scholastic attitude. In 1886 Charles F. Richardson, in his history of American Literature, put Thoreau into a chapter of minor essayists and said of him:

> He was the New England onlooker, the faithful chronicler of the woods, streams, fields, and skies of his world, that is to say the town of his birth . . . perpetually devoted to the woods and waters of his home. . . . This made him selfish, neglectful of his duties as a citizen and as a man among men, and, so far as his non-literary influence was concerned, of little use in the world. . . . His personal character was not large . . . in the character of Whitman are more largeness and light. . . . His chapters were like his days, merely separate parts of a serene and little-diversified life, free from the pleasures and restraints of a real home, remote from burning human hopes and strug-

gles, and, while caring much for the slave, caring little
for the country.

Thoreau's reputation survived that. Perhaps we should
mark that as the day he didn't die. But Richardson's attitude toward him didn't die either. In the last year of the
nineteenth century it was persisting with supercilious overtones in Barrett Wendell's *Literary History of America:*

> [The Thoreaus had] Yankee blood, but not of the socially
> distinguished kind . . . New England folks of the farming
> class, they had a kind of dogged self-assertive temper
> which inclined them to habits of personal isolation . . .
> As nobody was dependant on him for support, his method
> of life could do no harm . . . his eccentricity was not
> misanthropic. . . . He seems to have regarded his course
> as an experimental example. . . . If his life turned out
> well, others would ultimately imitate him; if it turned out
> ill, nobody else would be the worse . . . What gave him
> his lasting power was his unusually sympathetic observa-
> tion of nature . . . Nor is Thoreau's vitality in literature
> a matter only of his observation. Open his works almost
> anywhere . . . and even in the philosophic passages you
> will find loving precision of touch. . . . What is more,
> there can be no question that his speculations have ap-
> pealed to some very sensible minds. . . . Even their ad-
> mirers, however, must admit them to be colored
> throughout by the unflagging selfconsciousness involved in
> Thoreau's eccentric, harmless life . . . *Walden* remains
> a vital bit of literature for anyone who loves to read about
> Nature.

After all, we can forgive a Wendell for being a Brahmin;
but it is harder to understand how Julian W. Abernethy
(to whose library now at Middlebury we all owe a debt)
could have so conformed in the face of some of his friend-
ships and reading. Yet in 1902 this was his published
opinion of Thoreau:

> Reading and the study of wild life were the only occupa-
> tions that satisfied him, and for these he renounced the
> world . . . The neighboring farmers learned to respect
> the eccentric recluse . . . He had few friendships; ani-

mals and Indians were more companionable than cultivated men, because nearer the heart of Nature . . . His
master and chief friend was Emerson, the cast of whose
thought is on all he wrote. . . . The true value of Thoreau's writings has been discovered only in recent years.
The secret of his power is in a sympathetic and minute
knowledge of Nature, suffused with ideality.

This man they were writing about, believe it or not,
wrote "Civil Disobedience" and "Life Without Principle"
and "A Plea for Captain John Brown." He tried to wake
his neighbors up; but even as he was writing the last
paragraph of *Walden,* he feared that he had failed, that
neither John nor Jonathan would understand him, for his
light would be darkness to them. Sure enough, it was darkness to some Jonathans for, as we have just tallied it, a
full forty years.

It was John, not Jonathan, who saw the light first—the
Englishman, not the American. This may not be passing
strange. The prophet is honored outside his own country
sometimes for good reason. The other country may be
ready for him. At any rate, Dr. Alexander H. Japp began
in the 1870's to wonder whether Thoreau really was a man
—as he had read—of "morbid sentiment, weak rebellion,
and contempt for society." A little more reading and "a
self-sufficing but kindly and patriotic man took the place
of the 'morbid hermit.' . . . I wanted to find a reconciling
point." And by 1877, when he published *Thoreau, His
Life and Aims,* he had found the reconciling clue: "It was
Thoreau's love of nature that formed the basis of his
peculiar simplicity and dislike of what was involved,
doubtful, and tortuous: if we get to understand that, much
in his character which is otherwise puzzling, may become
clear to us." That may very well have been the dawning
of the day when Thoreau didn't die, for the spreading
British interest and growing insight into Thoreau's significance grew steadily after that: John Nichol's appraisal

in 1880, Robert Louis Stevenson's essay with Doctor Japp's corrective note the same summer, and the articles, editings, and biography by perhaps the best interpreter of all, Henry Salt, during the 1880's and 1890's.

John, then, discovered that Thoreau was much, much more than a Nature writer long before Jonathan did. Jonathan continued for another quarter century believing Lowell and Sanborn, Richardson and Barrett Wendell, seeing only a first-rate Nature writer, not puzzled by the other qualities of greatness which he could not see.

But even here, where Jonathan was so exasperatingly dull, one little nonacademic group had sharp insight and (stimulated by letters from across the Atlantic) circulating information, correcting errors, writing, photographing, printing, collecting, visiting, and interviewing, they slowly rescued Thoreau, not from his friends,—for Daniel Ricketson, H. G. O. Blake, and Thomas Wentworth Higginson should be credited with honest friendly service—but from his American biographers and literary historians.

A word should be spoken for that Concord dry-goods clerk, that Michigan doctor and his printer patient, that Ohio laborer, or (to name them) for Fred Hosmer, Doctor Samuel A. Jones, Edwin B. Hill, and Ernest Vickers. The day Thoreau didn't die in America was the day those men (and others whom they knew like the little group who met regularly in Buffalo with Charles S. Parke, or like Daniel Gregory Mason and his two friends at Harvard in 1898) decided to make the real Thoreau known, and as the best of amateurs set successfully about the evangel in the very nick of time, while old Concord still existed and scores of people who had known Thoreau still lived. Their dedicated working together in their crusade is one of the most thrilling behind-the-scenes "drives" I know of in literary history. We can't review it here. ["Some of the younger Americans," wrote Daniel Gregory Mason, "are beginning to realize that they have a great man in literature. It is a disgrace to this country that so true a son to it as Thoreau is unrecognized . . . We hope to help a little —sometime—in making him better understood."] It was as though they were converted men. ["The persistent misrepresentations of friends who insisted that Thoreau was 'this' or that he was not 'that', urging me to let him alone, only led me to read him the more," wrote Vickers, "with the result that I found him the deeper and nobler with the most superficial blemishes which vanished away as I came to know him still better."]

They themselves published next to nothing: a half dozen articles, twice as many brochures, and two thin books: *Thoreau: A Glimpse* and *Pertaining to Thoreau,* the latter printed one page at a time on a hand press evenings and Sundays at the expense of Edwin Hill's health. But they were "feeders" and correctors to those who did publish and edit—feeders of biographical facts, of bibliographical detail, of geographical data, of footnote accuracy. ["That," wrote Fred Hosmer, "will be as hard to fight against and correct as Emerson's trying to make Thoreau a 'perfect piece of stoicism.' " And Doctor Jones wrote, "After much correspondence, I get the following version . . . At last I am satisfied that the fact is as above stated."] For such things every one of us has been in their debt these three score years.

Last November, in quite another connection, a reviewer in the *New York Times* wrote: "It is a tribute to man's honesty and dogged hunt for truth that later generations have rediscovered, reassessed, and absorbed the work of these dissidents." In Thoreau's case it was not a generation, but a dozen men whom we must not forget at this centennial. They were a scattered little group of enthusiasts, but they had more than their share of honesty and dogged desire for truth about America's dissident. Encouraged by the dawn they saw break in England, they in America brought in the day when Thoreau didn't die.

J. LYNDON SHANLEY

Thoreau: Years of Decay and Disappointment?

"The mass of men lead lives of quiet desperation. What is called resignation is confirmed desperation. A stereotyped but unconscious despair is concealed under what are called the games and amusements of mankind. There is no play in them, for this comes after work. But it is a characteristic of wisdom not to do desperate things."

This is not only Thoreau's most notorious statement; it is also his fundamental charge against his fellow men. He repeated it in his books and essays, in his letters, and, one gathers, in his talk. On the other hand, he never ceased to assert that men should live with faith, hope, and love, because, he said, life was full of promise: "Men esteem truth remote, in the outskirts of the system, behind the farthest star, before Adam and after the last man. In eternity there is indeed something true and sublime. But all these times and places and occasions are now and here. God, himself, culminates in the present moment, and will never be more divine in the lapse of all ages."

The whirligig of time brings in its revenges: some thoughtful critics claim that Thoreau himself lost faith in the years after Walden Pond, wasted his time in fruitless work, and declined into the confirmed desperation called resignation:

Thoreau, isolated in America, his wits straying through the endless and utterly formless reaches of a transcendental Journal did not end his literary career as happily as Flaubert and Stevenson, . . . and Pater . . . ended theirs. That [his] main product was nothing, and his main effort vain, his own Journal best betrays.[1]

The last decade of Thoreau's life was "a decade of increasingly frequent crises, the testimony of which was all too clear in the thirteen *Journals* of the years from 1850 to 1861. These *Journals* record the desperation of the spiritual seeker who has lost his communion.[2]

A consecutive reading of the last portions of the *Journal* conveys the intolerable anguish of his sense "that there hath passed away a glory from the earth." By 1850 . . . he was already frightened. . . . By 1852 the agony is becoming intense. . . . Hence the fury . . . in 1853. . . . This was whistling to keep courage up, but toward the end he could hardly whistle.[3]

In support of these statements, the critics point primarily to the thirteen volumes of the *Journals* from 1850 to 1861. In them, Thoreau regrets that he has lost the ecstasy of his younger days and complains that scientific observation prevents him from experiencing Nature with his whole being. The critics see him as unsettled, unhappy, and drawn in opposite directions. And, they add, the *Journal* reflects his sad plight indirectly. Pages and pages of identifications, and lists of flora and fauna, and innumerable measurements are very dull stuff, and he who made them but never used them must have been desperately aware that he could never use them and that his work was coming to nothing. In addition, some claim that his philosophy was so unsound that it must inevitably have brought him to spiritual and emotional bankruptcy; finally, even *Walden* is offered as evidence of unhappiness.

[1] Mark Van Doren, *Henry David Thoreau, A Critical Study* (New York, 1916), pp. 84, 109.

[2] Sherman Paul, *The Shores of America* (Urbana, 1958), p. 256.

[3] Perry Miller, *Consciousness in Concord* (Boston, 1958), pp. 183–4.

There are other judgments, however, by other thoughtful critics:

Ecstasies were rare with him in these years, nostalgia for his more impressionable youth frequent, but the joy of free observation was constant. . . . For a man of his tastes, his temperament, and his philosophy, life had arranged itself ideally.[4]

The *Journal* is, after all, the most important part of the residuum of his life. . . . Here is a record of the use which he made of his time, of his sensibilities, and of his intelligence. And whatever the recording angel may think, whatever the posterity which remembers him may think, there seems to be no reasonable doubt that he himself regarded his life as a private success, however much it may have been a public failure. . . . there is no evidence that Thoreau ever found his life other than rewarding and sweet." [5]

My purpose is to show why I think these judgments right and the others wrong.

Of course, as he grew older, Thoreau found changes and losses as he compared the days of youth and of maturity; no reflective adult could fail to do so. William Butler Yeats, famous and admired, lamented at the age of forty-nine:

For some months now I have lived with my own youth and childhood . . . and I am sorrowful and disturbed . . . when I think of all the books I have read, and of the wise words I have heard spoken, and of the anxiety I have given to parents and grandparents, and of the hopes that I have had, all life weighed in the scales of my own life seems to me a preparation for something that never happens.[6]

Thoreau said: The youth gets together his materials to build a bridge to the moon . . . and at length the middle-

---

[4] Henry Seidel Canby, *Thoreau* (Boston, 1939), p. 333.

[5] Joseph Wood Krutch, *Henry David Thoreau* (New York, 1948), 145, 174.

[6] *The Autobiographies of W. B. Yeats* (New York, 1938), p. 94.

aged man concludes to build a wood-shed with them.
(July 14, 1852).

Wordsworth regretted in his ode:

It is not now as it hath been of yore;
Turn wheresoe'er I may
By night or day,
The things which I have seen I now can see no more.

And Thoreau said, "I think that no experience which I
have today comes up to, or is comparable with, the expe-
riences of my boyhood . . . my life was ecstacy. In youth
before I lost any of my senses, . . . I was alive. (July 16,
1851).

Thoreau watched his moods as narrowly as a cat does
a mouse; he noted his moments of nostalgia; they recurred
throughout the years. But they are only a minor theme,
it seems to me, in the vast journal record of a full and
satisfying life. And the complaint that observation and the
gathering of scientific data kept him from true experience
also recurs. There is no question that the complaint reflects
a difficulty, a conflict. It was an inevitable difficulty that
Thoreau's desire to know Concord and all its life drove
him to and that he accepted in action. If he was to know
Nature and her operations as he wanted to, he obviously
recognized that subjective experience must be comple-
mented by objective observation and records. He would
not rest content with "sublimo-slipshod" appreciation;
hence the long and frequent phenological lists; the measurements of snow depths, of rivers, and ponds; the counts
of tree rings. But, no more than the nostalgia for his youth,
does the occasional note of conflict between experience
and observation seriously affect the impression—produced
by myriad entries—of Thoreau forever searching and forever enjoying the search.

Consider how his regrets and complaints appear in the
journal entries of the first six months of 1853:

March 23, 1853: Man cannot afford to be a naturalist, to look at Nature directly, but only with the side of his eye. . . . I feel that I am dissipated by so many observations. . . . I have almost a slight, dry headache. . . . O for a little Lethe!

March 30, 1853: Ah, those youthful days! are they never to return? . . . No worm or insect, quadruped or bird, confined [my] view, but the unbounded universe was [mine]. A bird is now become a mote in [my] eye.

We cannot deny the dissatisfaction here, nor the disappointment in his relations with Emerson which he also recorded at this time.

Other entries in March, 1853, suggest a struggle to keep his spirits up: "All enterprises must be self-supporting, must pay for themselves. . . . You must get your living by loving." "Not only narrow but rough is the way that leadeth to life everlasting." ". . . Life is a battle in which you are to show your pluck, and woe be to the coward . . . despair and postponement are cowardice and defeat. Men were born to succeed, not to fail."[7]

But these notes can hardly be said to dominate the 368 pages of entries from January 1 to June 30, 1853. The major impression, as everywhere in the *Journals* from 1850 to 1861 is a fully engrossed Thoreau, ceaselessly observing and inquiring: we have lists of, notes on, questions about, and carefully worked descriptions of, natural phenomena; miscellaneous information—historical, economic, literary, architectural, etc.; comments on the manners and morals of the day; and sometimes set-pieces such as the account of the explosion of the Acton powder mill. And often— far more often than expressions of regret—we find expressions of Thoreau's pleasure in his work and the world he inhabited.

In January he delighted in the "crystal palace" created by the ice-sheathed trees and shrubs; in the "perfect

[7] March 13 and 21.

serenity and clarity and sonorousness in the earth" on a perfect winter morning; on another day he rejoiced in "an indescribably winter sky, pure and continent and clear, between emerald and amber, such as summer never sees!"[8]

In early March, after a day of riding about the country with a companion looking at farms, he commented: "I know of no more pleasing employment." On April 7th, eight days after one of his complaints about observations, he noted another side of the matter: "If you make the least correct observation of nature this year, you will have occasion to repeat it with illustrations the next, and the season and life itself is prolonged." On the same day he noted the beauty of the river at evening: "Nothing could be more elysian." In May he delighted in Alcott; and time and again he exclaimed at the loveliness of the earth: "How the air is saturated with sweetness on the causeways these willowy days," or ". . . that ineffable fragrance from the Wheeler meadow. . . . It is wafted from the garden of gardens," and "I was surprised, on turning around, to behold the serene and everlasting beauty of the world, it was so soothing . . . so much fairer, serener, more beautiful than my mood had been." And "The morning wind forever blows; the poem of the world is uninterrupted, but few are the ears that hear it." The same strain continues in June: "Here is home; the beauty of the world impresses you. There is a coolness in your mind as in a well. Life is too grand for supper." And, time after time, he states how his days are brightened by the beauty of wild roses, of water lilies, of a moonlit scene on the North River, by the songs of the blackbird or wood thrush, by the fragrance of the swamp pink.

These direct expressions of Thoreau's feelings in 1853

[8] For these and the undated entries of the following paragraph see, in the *Journals*, January 1, 3, 7, 20; March 8; May 9, 11, 17, 30; June 14, 15, 20, 22, 23.

are characteristic of those in the whole *Journal;* I think they reveal a happy man.

There remain, however, several hypothetical propositions that are offered to support the interpretation that he was unhappy.

Great stretches of the *Journal*, it is said, are formless and tedious masses of facts gathered according to an unsound scientific method; Thoreau never used most of them and never could have; therefore, the collecting of them must have been wearying and carried on out of sheer resignation.

Well—what would any seeker's unsifted and unorganized data be but formless and tedious to read, especially if one came upon them in a journal such as Thoreau's? And since he was not, and did not aspire to be, a scientist like Agassiz, the criticism that his method was not strictly scientific is beside the point. He wanted to know all Concord in his own way as, for example, he knew the ponds.

He saw his raw facts for what they were; he explained to his friend Blake why he could not give a lecture in Worcester in 1856: "In fine, what I have is either too scattered or loosely arranged, or too light, or else is too scientific and matter of fact (I run a good deal into that of late) for so hungry a company. I am still a learner, not a teacher, feeding somewhat omnivorously, browsing both stalk and leaves; but I shall perhaps be enabled to speak with the more precision and authority by and by,—if philosophy and sentiment are not buried under a multitude of details." [9]

Before he died, he had time to speak with authority only on fragments of his knowledge: the succession of forest trees, autumnal tints, and wild apples. As Emerson said: "The scale on which his studies proceeded was so

---

[9] *The Correspondence of Henry David Thoreau*, ed. Walter Harding and Carl Bode (New York, 1958), pp. 423–4.

large as to require longevity, and we were the less prepared for his sudden disappearance."[10]

The statement that Thoreau had prepared "agonies of assimilation" for himself[11] and could hardly have created order out of the mass of facts he had gathered can be countered by a simple question: "If you had read only the *Journals* from 1837 to 1854, could you imagine *Walden* made from them?" Of course, the question proves no more than the statement it counters. "What might have been is an abstraction/Remaining a perpetual possibility/Only in a world of speculation." We must remember, however, that, in addition to dull notes and lists, the *Journal* contains innumerable passages of vintage Thoreau, testifying to the vibrant spirit that impelled his unremitting search. "A hunger and a thirst are elements in his happiness and make it something other than mere content. And it is hunger and thirst which are responsible for the excitement of his writing."[12] Above all, we must not attribute the limits of our creative imagination to Thoreau.

Nor should we accept the following argument:

(1) A Romantic egoist is bound to be unhappy.

(2) Thoreau was an extreme Romantic egoist.

(3) Therefore, Thoreau was bound to be unhappy.

Since I believe the facts contradict the conclusion of the syllogism, the argument might be dismissed out-of-hand; but I think something more should be said. This is no time to explore the major premise: that is, the humanists' judgment on the happiness of Romantic egoists. I would, however, question the minor premise: the judgment that Thoreau was so arrogant a Romantic egoist as to have been headed "as recklessly as Tamburlaine or Faust toward catastrophe,"[13] or that he "went a step be-

---

[10] "Biographical Sketch" in Henry D. Thoreau, *Excursions* (Boston, 1863), p. 33.

[11] Paul, *op. cit.*, p. 114.

[12] Krutch, *op. cit.*, p. 215.

[13] Miller, *op. cit.*, p. 34.

yond Emerson's mad (but manly) intellectual egoism,"[14] and was therefore doomed to despair. Against these statements I would place that of no less a critic of Romantic egoism than Paul Elmer More; he concluded his analysis of Thoreau and the German Romantic thinkers in this fashion: "The freedom of the romantic school was to the end that the whole emotional nature might develop; in Thoreau it was for the practice of a higher self-restraint. . . . And so, despite its provincialism and its tedium, the *Journal* of Thoreau is a document that New England may cherish proudly. . . . there remains this tonic example of a man who did actually and violently break through the prison walls of routine, and who yet kept a firm control of his career."[15]

Finally, *Walden* itself, one of the gayest of books, is offered as evidence of unhappiness. Professor Perry Miller characterizes the description of the thawing sandbank in "Spring" as "this ultimate—this derisive, tortured—irony at the end of *Walden*."[16] Since I cannot understand this reading, I cannot argue: in terms of the famous *New Yorker* cartoon, one of us sees broccoli, the other spinach. Or in more philosophical terms: *De gustibus et de coloribus non est disputandum.*

I can argue, however, against Professor Paul's use of *Walden* as evidence (supplementary to that of the *Journal*) of Thoreau's unhappiness after 1850.

He states that the experiment at Walden was effective and that Thoreau "renewed his faith by living there and by writing the *Week.*" The cure was not lasting, however, and *Walden*, he continues, was "an attempt to drain the cup of inspiration to its last dregs. Whatever its public intention, its personal intention was therapeutic."[17]

[14] Van Doren, *op. cit.*, p. 34.
[15] "Thoreau's Journal" in *Selected Shelburne Essays* (New York, 1935), pp. 114-16.
[16] Miller, *op. cit.*, p. 127.
[17] Paul, *op. cit.*, pp. 234, 294.

The development of this point of view suffers from a serious error: it assumes that *Walden* did not finally get under way until after 1850, and it therefore offers as evidence of Thoreau's reaction to his alleged unhappiness in 1850–54 a number of classic passages that he wrote in the first version of *Walden* in 1846–47.

(1) The *Journals* from 1850 to 1861 "record the desperation of the spiritual seeker who has lost his communion and full explain the sense of loss which Thoreau intended to convey in the allegorical passage in the hound, the bay-horse, and the turtledove."

(2) "To anticipate, not the sunrise and the dawn merely, but, if possible, Nature herself . . . expressed the enterprise of his years of decay."

(3) ". . . as his allusion to Hebe indicated, he was advising a cure for himself as well as his neighbors. Open all your pores to nature, live in all the seasons—these had been the injunctions of his years of decay."

(4) "With these losses [failure to achieve social influence, failure of the *Week* to sell] for his background, he described for the first time his purpose in going to Walden in a passage [trade with the Celestial Empire, "Economy,"] that brilliantly fused the imagery of self-reliance and spiritual recovery with that of commerce." [18]

But all four passages were in the Walden of 1846–47; they cannot be offered as evidence of Thoreau's reaction to despair and decay in 1850–54. [19]

At the end of his explication of *Walden*, Professor Paul presents the ecstatic climax of what he calls the therapeutic—as well as literary—myth of rebirth that Thoreau's alleged unhappiness led him to create.

> The ecstasy [of the passage on the thawing sand at the railroad cut] was not spontaneous or unconscious, but

[18] *Ibid.*, pp. 256, 321, 327, 323.
[19] "The First Version of *Walden*," pp. 113, 169, 114–15, in J. Lyndon Shanley, *The Making of Walden* (Chicago, 1957).

intellectual; it followed from his mature study of nature and his perception of law, an ecstatic praise of this guarantee in nature, but not the former ecstasy he was seeking . . . as an example of his conscious endeavor in nature it represented the intellectual basis from which the more successful symbols of ecstasy—the melting pond and the soaring hawk—were struck.[20]

He then summarizes paragraph thirteen, "The first sparrow of spring," and fourteen, "Walden is melting apace"; quotes almost all of fifteen, "The change from storm and winter to serene and mild"; summarizes the joys of the Golden Age; and presents the soaring, tumbling hawk, in paragraph twenty-two, as the final symbol of Thoreau's ultimate liberation.

But these "more successful symbols of ecstasy" were not born of despair in 1850–54; nor were they struck off after the full development, in 1853–54, of the long passage on the thawing sand. Thoreau wrote "The first sparrow of spring," "The change from storm and winter to serene and mild," and the description of the hawk in the *Walden* of 1846–47.[21] He kept them for the published version of *Walden* and added other material later, not because he had to fend off despair, but because their ecstasy expressed his never failing belief in the promise of life, and also gave proof of its fulfillment.

In 1852–53, Thoreau added the following passage to *Walden:* "I learned this, at least, by my experiment; that if one advances confidently in the direction of his dreams, and endeavors to live the life which he has imagined, he will meet with a success unexpected in common hours." I do not think Thoreau ever forgot the lesson he learned while living at Walden Pond. Those who knew him testified to his success. Immediately after Thoreau's death, a young Harvard student wrote:

[20] Paul, *op. cit.*, pp. 349–51.
[21] "The First Version," pp. 204–6.

He appeared to us more than all men to enjoy all life
. . . for its intrinsic worth, taking great interest in everything connected with the welfare of the town, no less than
delight in each changing aspect of Nature, with an instinc-
tive love for every creature of her realm.

And his family told Mary Peabody Mann "they never
could be sad in his presence for a moment; he had been
the happiest person they had ever known, all through
his life." [22]

And so, as he lay dying, Thoreau could say he was not
aware that he and God had ever quarreled. We can regard
this as flippant irreverence only if we take the lament of
Job for the whole truth, and forget the happiness of the
psalmist. Thoreau did not. He loved to quote: "Tomorrow
to fresh woods and pastures new." As far as he was concerned, God had always given him "green pastures."

[22] *Thoreau, Man of Concord,* ed. Walter Harding (New York, 1960),
pp. 11–12, 114.

REGINALD L. COOK

A Parallel of Parablists: Thoreau and Frost

1.

Henry Thoreau and Robert Frost are attached by lineal descent to a native story-telling tradition. The parable is the literary form by which they give this tradition an original twist. Yet sharply separated as they are in time and temperament, in a sense they are complementary parablists. The ligament that joins is far stronger than the epochs which separate them. In 1954 during the *Walden* centenary, Robert Frost taped a radio script which was released on the B.B.C. Home Service. Plumping for *Walden* as a tale of adventure, a declaration of independence, and a gospel of wisdom, he referred to it as one of the three books (the other two are *Robinson Crusoe* and *The Voyage of the Beagle*) that had "a special shelf in [his] heart." He identified Thoreau's chief theme as "a freedom within freedom," and he contended Thoreau's affinity for freedom was not a desire for liberty "with a capital L." Frost said of Thoreau: "He was not interested in the liberty brightest in dungeons and on the scaffold as much as he was in the daily liberties he could take right under the noses of the high and mighty and the small and petty." Resourcefully keeping snug within the admitted limits of time, place, and form, Frost declares his own

independence "from the modern pace." These three ties—
the readability of *Walden*, "freedom within freedom," and
the counterfriction to the contemporary speed-up—reflect
Frost's "Thorosian" (his own coinage) affinity.

Thoreau's typical parable is aspiratory; Frost's is speculative. Each reflects his epoch. Thoreau's parables are
marked by introspective idealism, a mood not uncharac-
teristic of the Transcendentalists. There is an appealing
moral perfectionism in the parable of Kouroo and more
than a touch of nostalgic idealism in the lost bay horse,
turtle dove, and hound. Frost's parables are commonly an
imaginative means of objectifying *felt* experience in our
sharply realistic era.

As a Transcendentalist, Thoreau usually originates his
parable in a correspondence between the data of sense
and spirit. Like Emerson, his world was emblematic, and
he associated "the laws of ethics" with natural phenomena
like the song of the thrush, robin or bay-wing; the full-
veined, well-tanned shrub oak leaf; snow crystals; wild
apples; river reflections; a flock of lesser red polls; or the
saunterer's herb-garden on the old settlers' road. The
passionate life he lived in nature was meticulously translated into the insights of the metaphoric parables. So it is
that he hoed diligently in his bean-field, certainly not
because he subscribed to an economy of beans, but "for
the sake of tropes and expression, to serve a parable-maker
one day." Indeed, it was his custom to hoe symbolic bean-
fields, climb symbolic mountains, walk into symbolic
sunset worlds (as at Spaulding's Farm), measure the depth
of symbolic ponds. The envelope of his parable is natural
phenomena, and the nuclear symbol is a pilgrimage—a
venturing of the spirit. His "constitutionals" in the Concord ambit became not only the source of his parables but
symbolic of them.

Yeats' assertion that "the more unconscious the creation
the more powerful" applies to Thoreau's parables. Let us

see how this is true. There are, for example, the conscious parables which appear in his *Journals:* the parable of the man of reason and the habitual thinker (March 4, 1852); the parable of the flailer (August 29, 1854); and a midwinter transcendental parable that fairly out-transcendentalizes Alcott, which might appropriately be entitled "On the track of the Great Hare" (January 1, 1854). Then there is the conscious parable on the right way to climb a mountain, which he rather ironically sent to Harrison Blake *after* the latter had returned from a trip to the White Mountains. He thought climbing to the top of Mt. Washington and being blown on was nothing. He wanted to know, "What did the mountain say? What did the mountain do?" Careful to follow his own gratuitous counsel, he parablized to Blake: "I keep a mountain anchored off eastward a little way, which I ascend in my dreams both awake and asleep. Its broad base spreads over a village or two, which do not know it; neither does it know them, nor do I when I ascend it. I can see its general outline as plainly now in my mind as that of Wachusett. I do not invent in the least, but state exactly what I see. I find that I go up it when I am light-footed and earnest. It even smokes like an altar with its sacrifices. I am not aware that a single villager frequents it or knows it. I keep this mountain to ride instead of a horse." What could be more symbolic than a mountain that "serves us like an altar with its sacrifices?" The ascent is no matter-of-fact hike: to climb the mythical mountain requires moral as well as physical energy. Moreover, it is real to the inward eye. It is to be believed in with conviction. Symbolic of a personal aspiration, it is an ideal which a poet keeps to ride like a horse on the days he does not ascend Wachusett, Monadnock, Ktaadn, Mt. Washington, Ponkawtasset, or the Fair Haven cliffs.

Thoreau's counsel to Blake has a background. In the *Journal*, under the entry for October 29, 1857, a little over two weeks before he wrote Blake, he mentions a parable-like dream which had recurred to him "for the twentieth time at least" over a period of years. In the dream he is always climbing a mountain in the easterly part of the town, "where," as he says, "no high hill actually is." En route he passes through the gate at the Burying-Hill without being aware of the concealed graves. There are two ways up the mountain. One is through the dark woods and the other is through a sunny pasture. His customary approach to the top is through dark, unfrequented woods at the base—a fact which bothers him because the summit is quite as accessible through a sunny pasture. In the ascent he passes along a rocky ridge, haunted by wild beasts, where the trees are stunted. He shudders as he struggles upward, until, passing an imaginary line, he loses himself in the upper air and clouds at the summit, which is "unhandselled, awful, grand." When, in his thoughts, he has climbed the mountain he is always surprised as he looks off between the mists at the summit, to see "how it is ever adjacent to [his] own native fields."

The effect of the ascent is momentous. "It can never become familiar; you are lost the moment you set foot there," he says, emphatically. "You know no path, but wander, thrilled, over the bare and pathless rock, as if it were solidified air and rock." Invariably the pleasure he takes in this climb is tinged with awe, and, most important of all, his thoughts are purified and sublimated, "as if [he] had been translated." In view of Thoreau's Transcendental aspirations, this is certainly an instructive parable-like dream. It hardly requires a gloss, but the pairings are notable. There are such antimonies as the dark and the sunny, the far and the near, the awe-filling and the pleasurable, the wild and the cultivated, the melancholy and the thrilling, the concealed death and the apparent life. Above all, there is the uniqueness of the experience. "It can never become familiar." And, on reflection, he recalls he felt just as the Puritans did when they experienced grace—"as if I had been *translated*," he says [my italics]. Thoreau is not always ascending mythical mountains. He is as alert to the possibilities of the common view as he is to the Pisgah view. An interesting little parable grew out of the excursion on the Concord and Merrimac rivers with his brother John in 1839. When they came to Billerica, the idea of the settling of a New England town stirred his imagination and the picture he evokes has implications similar to those we find in the more obvious parables. I think it valid to call this imaginative account a parable, because, as we see, it is really a composite vision of many New England towns—my own, for example, which was less than thirty miles away—and Thoreau does underscore the implication in his account. Furthermore, does this not reflect aspects of Yeats' assertion that "the more unconscious the creation the more powerful?"

In *A Week* he says: "Some spring the white man came, built him a house, and made a clearing here, letting in the sun, dried up a farm, piled up the old gray stones in fences, cut down the pines around his dwelling, planted orchard seeds brought from the old country, and persuaded the civil apple tree to blossom next to the wild pine and the juniper. . . . He culled the graceful elm from out the woods and from the river-side, and so refined and smoothed his village plot. And thus he plants a town. He rudely bridged the stream, and drove his team afield into the river meadows, cut the wild grass, and laid bare the homes of beaver, otter, muskrat, and with the whetting of his scythe scared off the deer and bear. He set up a mill, and fields of English grain sprang in the virgin soil. And with his grain he scattered the seeds of the dandelion and the wild trefoil over the meadows, mingling his English flowers with the wild native ones. . . ."

As Thoreau says: clearing, draining, lumbering, building, fencing, planting, "the white man comes, pale as the dawn, with a load of thought, with a slumbering intelligence as a fire raked up, knowing well what he knows, not guessing but calculating; strong in community, yielding obedience to authority; of experienced race; of wonderful, wonderful common sense; dull but capable, slow but persevering, severe but just, of little humor but genuine; a laboring man, despising game and sport; building a house that endures, a framed house. He buys the Indian's moccasins and baskets, then buys his hunting grounds, and at length forgets where he is buried, and plows up his bones. And here town records, old, tattered, timeworn, weatherstained chronicles, contain the Indian sachem's mark, perchance an arrow or a beaver, and the few fatal words by which he deeded his hunting grounds away. He comes with a list of ancient Saxon, Norman, and Celtic names, and strews them up and down this river,—Framingham, Sudbury, Bedford, Carlisle, Billerica, Chelmsford,—and this is New Angle-land, and these are the new West Saxons, whom the red men call, not Angle-ish or English, but Yengeese, and so at last they are known for Yankees."

Although there is in Thoreau's imaginative account of the settlement of a New England town no such dialectic as we find frequently in Frost, the moral implication goes as directly to the heart of the Thoreauvian ethic as the implications do in Frost's speculative parables. Thoreau muses on the village and sums up the point of the parallelism. "Every one," he says, "finds by his own experience, as well as in history that the era in which men cultivate the apple, and the amenities of the garden, is essentially different from that of the hunter and forest life, and neither can displace the other without loss." We shall keep in mind this little parable of the white man planting a civilization in a wilderness area inhabited by aborigines and turn to *Walden*, unfortunately, for only the briefest glance.

Walden is Thoreau's classic parable. "Thoreau's immortality may hang by a single book," as Robert Frost says, "but the book includes even his writing that is *not* in it. Nothing he ever said but sounds like a quotation from it." This is perhaps true of any writer's masterpiece. *Walden* confirms Yeats' statement about "the more unconscious creation." Independence, which was central in Thoreau's life, is unconsciously expressed in the part as well as in the whole. He was never, for instance, more independent than when he sat in his sunny Walden doorway from sunrise till noon, "rapt in a revery." *Walden* is a parable of self-realization, as powerful in this respect as it is unconsciously so. It reflects the struggle for and attainment of self-realization on the following levels: economic (the chapters on "Economy" and "The Bean-Field"); intellectual (the chapters on "Where I Lived" and "Reading"); moral (the chapters on "Solitude" and "Higher Laws"); social (the chapters on "Visitors" and "Winter Visitors"); and psychological (the chapters entitled "Solitude" and "Conclusion"). The essence of Thoreau's parable is a spiritual pilgrimage. The natural world to which he responded with the intimacy of sympathy and understanding is a spirit-infused world. "I am thankful," he says, "that this pond was made deep and pure for a symbol." From the early spring of 1845, when he cut down the pines for his shelter on the shores of Walden Pond, through the summer of the bean-field and the winter of the ice-makers at Walden, until the next spring, we follow the seasons inwardly as well as outwardly. The record recapitulates a life-death cycle. "Walden was dead and is alive again." So, too, is the human spirit. Like the grass blades, "our human life but dies down to its root, and still puts forth its green blade to eternity."

2.

But what does Robert Frost reflect of the parablist? "A parable," he says, "is a story that means what it says and something besides, and according to the New Testament, the 'something besides' is the more important of the two." Like Thoreau, as we have noted, he belongs to the native story-telling tradition, especially with his emphasis on concrete details, a relaxed presentation, and a colloquial idiom. If he had been content to repeat an inherited tradition, he might only be considered a regional yarnspinner in verse. But in a teasing, oblique, ruminative way, he gives the commonplace an uncommon twist in expression, using a method which Goethe has described. "If a man grasps the particular vividly," says Goethe, "he also grasps the general, without being aware of it at the time; or he may make the discovery long afterwards." This is Frost's method in "The Demiurge's Laugh" and "The Tuft of Flowers," in "Range-Finding" and "A Star in a Stone-Boat," in "Birches" and "After Apple-Picking," in "Directive" and "West Running Brook," in "The Grindstone" and "The Wood-Pile," in "The Code" and "A Cabin in the Clearing." In his parable-like poems, either lyric or narrative, serious or humorous in tone, the idea is released through an incident "common in experience."

"The Demiurge's Laugh,"* from *A Boy's Will*, has been selected because it is short and typical. In context the demiurge, or "the Demon," implies a subordinate deity, not the supreme God. This important distinction influences the interpretation of the poem. Here is the poem:

> It was far in the sameness of the wood;
>   I was running with joy on the Demon's trail,
> Though I knew what I hunted was no true god.
>   It was just as the light was beginning to fail
> That I suddenly heard—all I needed to hear:
> It has lasted me many and many a year.
>
> The sound was behind me instead of before,
>   A sleepy sound, but mocking half,

As of one who utterly couldn't care.
The Demon arose from his wallow to laugh,
Brushing the dirt from his eye as he went;
And well I knew what the Demon meant.

I shall not forget how his laugh rang out.
I felt as a fool to have been so caught,
And checked my steps to make pretence
It was something among the leaves I sought
(Though doubtful whether he stayed to see.)
Thereafter I sat me against a tree.

Significantly the first stanza shows us how deeply affected the protagonist is by what he hears while he runs with joy on the trail of "no true god" in the stretch of woods, "just as the light was beginning to fail." What does this mean? Is this little scene to be taken factually or symbolically? Unmistakably a parable, rather than a dream or a fantasy, the poem is saying one thing in terms of another.

The first stanza introduces the situation. The second stanza tells us what happens. The protagonist in pursuit of the Demon is suddenly startled by a drowsy, mocking laugh from behind. The wily Demon has outwitted him by rising unexpectedly from its wallow, drowsily to mock the protagonist, who now is certain he knows "what the Demon meant."

Whatever the enigmatic laugh means to us—if it is supposed to mean anything specific—it is at least apparent what its effect is on the protagonist. The mocking laugh convicted him, and he "felt a fool to have been so caught." Reacting humanly he pretends it is something else and not the Demon he is seeking. "And checked my steps to make pretence. It was something among the leaves I sought."

This short poetic parable is the sharper for withheld inobvious meaning. But the essentials are here: the object of the search, the seeker's attitude, the occasion of his being taken in, and the dawn of self-awareness. The untrue god can stand for any suspect motivation; for example, the fashionable doctrines of a lesser faith, hedonistic appetite, or possibly devotion to Darwinian science as the key to the universe. A parable hints; the reader supplies the meaning for the counters. This particular parable does not aim to contrast ignorance and enlightenment. The protagonist is clear eyed. He knows what he hunts is "no true god." Exuberant willfulness or the contrariness of lusty youth—not ignorance—seems a closer clarification of the motive. The bite here is felt by those who follow a suspect god and get "taken," as Frost seizes and dramatizes the all-too-human predisposition to ignore our better impulses. Until the moment of exposure we give our unrestrained impulses free rein and joyously pursue demons. Then, chagrined and smarting from the effect of our callowness, we stop to think it over. In the candor of defeat we admit: "Thereafter I sat me against a tree."

The dominant motile image of the chase is deepened and given scope by the unvarying landscape—"the sameness of the wood." It is dramatized sharply by the unpleasant personification of the disheveled Demon, rising from his wallow and "brushing the dirt from his eye as he went." Isn't it precisely in this negative way that Darwinism, with its inversion of angels and apes, startled the secular piety of the nineteenth century? The image of "the failing light" re-enforces this interpretation. Objects become ambiguous; the Demon slips behind the protagonist. And failing light suggests the dimming of faith, or at least human unsureness of the reality of objects. The main incident, like Goodman Brown's *Walpurgis Nacht,* is completely enveloped in the natural world, in the depths of the dark woods. The parable opens by focussing our attention on the interminable woods; it closes by directing our eye toward a particular tree. What of the significance of Nature? Nature is inescapable but it isn't necessarily malevolent. Its enticing demiurges are mischievous and repelling but not vicious. Set your back to Nature and think over what has happened.

3.

In this parallel of parablists exactly where do Thoreau and Frost differ? Thoreau's most characteristic parable embodies aspirative perfectionism. This attitude is glimpsed in the parable of Kouroo, and in the dreamlike parable of the mountain climb, and even in the cryptic parable of the loss of the bay-horse, the turtle dove and the hound, which, according to Emerson, referred respectively to Thoreau's desire for property, the wife of his dreams, and the book he would have written. His dominant mode is the evocative excursus of the lyric statement in an expository passage. And in tone there is often a tinge of nostalgia for the way it was, as we note in the Billerica parable, or in the fleeting vision of the town from the mountain top.

In Frost's parable-like poems the essential characteristic is a play of mind. Such a play requires verbal agility. Since play and counterplay for Frost are the heart of poetry, a poem is, by his definition, "a trial by agility." So speculative is his dialectical play of mind, critics are convinced the constant shifting of position in his relationship to experience invites the charge of evasiveness. Evasive or not, Frost's dominant mode is dramatic. There is commonly a dramatic give-and-take in his poems, either between specific protagonists or within the poet.

There is also a difference in temperament and method of approach. Strenuous in his journey-mindedness, Thoreau's parables reflect an intimate, passional intensity. He is in earnest about his journeys. He works at them. They represent an effort to establish a correspondence between Nature and himself. Frost is more relaxed than Thoreau, although perhaps not less deliberate. His dynamic equilibrium reflects a free rather than a systematic exploration of experience. A constant vigilance accounts for the continuous dialectical act of intelligence apparent within the texture of his parables. Invariably the movement, as in "Birches," "A Drumlin Woodchuck," and "Directive," is one of withdrawal and return. Alternation is the key to the cyclic movement. "That would be good both going and coming back," he says in "Birches." Moving cautiously and shrewdly from the data of the senses, he appeals to the head as well as the heart. The idea comes to a crisis *in* the parable and not in a statement about the crisis. Natural insight suffices, which is, as some think, a major limitation in the poet's viewpoint. In Blake and Yeats natural insight is not enough; they exalt a fourfold vision. In Yeats, for example, at a point beyond reality vision is concretely embodied. But, like Yeats, you have to wear an embroidered coat of myth to grasp this vision. Frost's flights are horizontal, his range terrestrial, his virtue courage, his religion self-dependence.

Obviously Thoreau and Frost do differ in kinds of parables, temperament, modes of expression, subject matter, and method. We would expect this. But a more fundamental difference originates in their vision of reality. Thoreau's universe is a moral one where the sanctions are divine, and where we are aware—as in his journal references —of "the mind of the universe" intended upon such commonplaces of the natural world as the ash-colored cocoons of the Promethea moth on a buttonbush, or the leaves of the Norway cinquefoil closing protectively over its seeds.

The ethic of a Thoreauvian parable is, in consequence, based upon moral insights. We recall that Thoreau's symbolic mountain climb affected him "as if [he] had been translated." We remember also that the mythical white man who came to New England effected the changes that transformed a wilderness area into Billerica only by dint of a moral athleticism.

In our positivistic epoch, the ethic of Thoreau's parables might be regarded as the compulsive fulfilment of a strenuous impulse to read moral purposiveness *into* natural phenomena and human effort. Frost projects another vision of reality. In his relationship to experience he is skeptical of ultimate answers. In one of his later poems, entitled "The Most of It," when the protagonist shouts across the woodland lake, the only sound he hears is the mocking echo of his own voice. Frost is suggesting there is no original response—no counterlove—in nature; there is only the great buck, which "powerfully appeared" from the water and stumbled through the rocks with horny tread, "and forced the under-brush—and that was all." The finality of "and that was all" marks the separation of Frost's skepticism from Thoreau's prehensions of correspondence with the "mind of the universe." A world of ideological difference here divides the two parablists.

The fact is Frost has no preformed conviction, no prejudgment, except as he trusts his reason. The source of his wisdom is a judgment *after* the fact. Insofar as man does feel something beyond or in and through things, this is admissible reality. Frost's reality is objective; that is, it has an autonomous existence correlative with himself. But there is no "mystique" attached to it. It is, however, a substantial recommendation that in the levelness of Frost's vision—which is not to be equated with an inability to respond with warrantable enthusiasm—there is a refusal to see more than is to be seen. Nature is contemplated by Frost with becoming detachment.

4.

"The development of modern art with its seemingly nihilistic trend toward disintegration must be understood as the symptom and symbol of a mood of world destruction and world renewal that has set its mark on our age," says Carl Jung. The master image for this mood and trend is "the waste land," but it is to be doubted that America's poet-at-large, Robert Frost, has been willing to acknowledge the Eliot image as central or world destruction as inevitable. Like Thoreau, he emphasizes renewal. Those who see the dark side in Frost are not astigmatic; there are more than a few square rods of Eliot's waste land implied in "A Servant to Servants," "The Housekeeper," "Home Burial," "Design," "Acquainted with the Night," and "Hill Wife." Frost recognizes evil, but mostly it is man made. The problem whether the human spirit can be at home in the universe is not really so fundamental as under what conditions it chooses to survive. At present a sense of estrangement has not nullified the fact that man still supports himself in an alien universe. Alienation rather than negating human responsibility only serves to intensify the capacity of human endurance. "No choice is left a poet . . .," Frost has said, "but how to take the curse, tragic or comic?" He takes it a little both ways, without blaming our plight on some vague force beyond our ken. In a century when shadows of menacing events strike across our path, he evokes at times gaily, at times mockingly and satirically, a comic vision of limitation in the human condition. Similarly, he reflects the tragic "tears in things," which come from an awareness of grief and misery, sorrow and despair. As "a good Greek" he might nod approvingly at Santayana's statement: "Weep, my son, if you are human, but laugh also, if you are a man."

I shall close on the note resonantly struck by both. It is the note of freedom—the freedom Thoreau exercises in his inclination to climb symbolic mountains and Frost to stay snug but operative within the admitted limits of form, tradition, human relationship, nationalism. While Thoreau is primarily interested in testing freedom and arbitrary authority, Frost is interested in the tension between freedom and *natural* limits. Thoreau is concerned with curbing authority and mastering circumstance, so that by saving on the lower levels he might the better spend on the higher. There's a good deal of concern with self-realization in Thoreau. Frost has been interested, enterprising, and ingenious in finding ways and means "to be free in harness," as he says, or "to swing his load" of knowledge and experience with consummate ease; that is, to attain a maximum of independence for imaginative thrusts in a minimum of constricting limits. His ultimate aim is, of course, to make from this challenge and struggle "little bits of clarity." "Little bits of clarity" is precisely what both Yankees have succeeded in giving us in their parables. Each has dramatized the terms of man's appeal from cosmic insignificance: Thoreau in terms of his intense moral perfectionism, and Frost in terms of his "passionate preferences."

HOWARD MUMFORD JONES

Thoreau and
Human Nature*

On Sunday, May 5, 1962, with appropriate
ceremony Henry David Thoreau was, on the centenary
of his death, formally admitted to the Hall of Fame in
New York City. To his admirers over the world this seemed
not only an appropriate action, but an action too long
delayed. If Thoreau has not exerted an influence quite
comparable to that of James Fenimore Cooper or Edgar
Allan Poe, he has exerted an international influence that
has increased in the twentieth century; and this influence,
moreover, has been an influence of action, as in India
or among our own Freedom Riders, and not an influence
solely of literature and thought. It will in no way reflect
upon the justice of his admission or upon the good sense
of the jury that selected Thoreau to speculate on what he
might have said, were he alive today and aware of the
honor.

He hated cities, he hated museums, and he hated statuary. In September, 1843, he wrote in his *Journal:* "I
walked through New York yesterday—and met no real or
living person." In another, undated entry in a notebook
he said: "I hate museums; there is nothing so weighs upon
my spirits. They are the catacombs of nature." And in
1859, when somebody asked him to subscribe for a statue

* Reprinted with permission from the *Atlantic Monthly,* CCX (September, 1962), 56–61, and from *History and the Contemporary* (Madison,
University of Wisconsin Press, 1964).

to Horace Mann, he declined, thinking that a man "ought not any more to take up room in the world after he was dead. . . . It is very offensive to my imagination to see the dying stiffen into statues at this rate." Eulogies and statuary are perhaps necessary, however, and one may hope they are the outward and visible sign of our inward and spiritual grace.

I am not a Thoreau specialist. I am not expert in Thoreau's reading, which was immense, nor in his economic views, if he had any, nor in his love life, which seems to have been meager and problematical, nor have I participated in the battle—dare one say, of the ants?—that has raged over the exact location of the famous hut on Walden Pond. But what does one find on rereading Thoreau?

One general image it is difficult to confirm. I can best express this image by citing two sentences with which Leo Stoller begins his study of Thoreau's economic views. He writes: "Henry Thoreau is the man who lived alone in a hut by Walden Pond and went to jail rather than pay taxes. Such, at any rate, is the thumbnail sketch of him by an American eager to tolerate what he considers primitivism and oddity." Mr. Stoller does not say this image is correct; he merely gives it as a sketch of popular belief. Neither branch of the legend seems to be quite true. Thoreau went to jail only once for failing to pay his taxes; he did not protest when they were paid for him; and Sam Staples, the town jailer, said he was mad as the devil at being locked up.

As for living an eremite's life in a sort of primitive wilderness by Walden, this, too, will not quite do. Thoreau went there July 4, 1845, and it was theoretically his home for two years and two months. But he had to abandon it from Wednesday, November 12th, to Saturday, December 6th, because, not having plastered the hut in warm weather, he had to go home until the plaster had slowly dried. Dur-

ing the second summer he took a by no means solitary trip
to the Maine woods. In good weather he went to Concord
almost daily, sometimes lingering there into the night,
going either to look after his family and see his friends
or to do odd jobs for pay. In good weather, likewise, he
was frequently visited by friends, neighbors, Transcendentalists, curiosity seekers, and even young ladies. In the
winter he had the companionship of the ice cutters, which
he seems to have enjoyed, and in the fall, particularly, that
of hunters, one group of whom he characterizes as a
"numerous and merry crew."

Of the eighteen chapters into which *Walden* is di-
vided, the first and longest, entitled "Economy" (in the
Greek sense), is as much social commentary as it is directions on how to build a cabin and plant beans. Another
is entitled "Visitors." Another describes a visit to the Baker
farm and chronicles a chat with its inhabitants. Another
is entitled "The Village"—"that desperate, odd-fellow
society," he calls it. Chapter Fourteen is a kind of Robert
Frost commentary upon present and former residents and
frequenters of the area.

One scholarly editor of *Walden* insists that Chapter
Four, on "Sounds," may be a lesson in how to read the
universal, living language of Nature. I am not disposed
to dispute this philosophical assertion or to pretend to be
deaf to the "native wood-notes wild" held suspended in
its exquisitely modulated prose. But of the twenty-two
paragraphs that make up the chapter, nine are devoted
to or take off from the noises made by the railroad trains,
one has to do with the "faint rattle of a carriage or team
along the distant highway," one is occasioned by hearing
the church bells of Lincoln, Acton, Bedford, and Concord,
one combines the distant lowing of a cow with a satirical
passage on some village lads singing. The penultimate
paragraph begins with another distant rumbling of wagons
over bridges, the baying of farm dogs, and the lowing of

another cow; and the final one opens with a meditation on crowing roosters, a sound, says Thoreau, heard round the world, even on sailing ships. Sounds are sounds, and aural acuity—Thoreau had sensitive ears—can be as well displayed by recording the rumble of a team over a bridge as by recording the language of an aldermanic frog as *tr-r-r-oonk, tr-r-r-oonk, tr-r-r-oonk,* but the ordinary reader may be forgiven if he is baffled when told that this not very original onomatopoeia is a new lesson in the universal, living language of Nature.

I note also with mild amusement that Chapter Five, entitled "Solitude," contains phrases like these: "I find that visitors have been there"; "I was frequently notified of the passage of a traveller along the highway sixty rods off by the scent of his pipe"; "some came from the village to fish for pouts"; "men frequently say to me"; "I one evening overtook one of my townsmen." Wiser than specialists, Thoreau says flatly in *Walden* that we belong to the community.

I think he went to Walden Pond in part to get away from his garrulous mother, in part to meditate and write, but he was no solitary Alexander Selkirk, no monarch of all he surveyed, no Robinson Crusoe discovering with astonishment on the sand a print of a human foot, no Trappist monk dedicated to silence, no St. Anthony trying to be holy in the desert. He built his hut and he lived in it because it was fun to do so. I have known Vermonters who lived far more solitary lives in far more lonely dwellings.

A man maun gang his ain gait, as the Scots say, without being a solitary in either the romantic or the religious sense. On rereading other books by Thoreau I am astonished to see how large a fraction of their bulk is devoted to commentary on humanity. *A Week on the Concord and Merrimack Rivers* runs to 518 pages, of which about 200 have to do directly with the journeying. Both streams run—and ran—through territory long since subdued to human needs, and the pages deal with farm and church, canal and bridge, lock and village, factory and stagecoach, river commerce and social history. He or his brother ever and again hails canalboat men or farmers or small boys or lockkeepers or hospitable farmwives.

Their little trip, in itself charming, was quite without wildness, and could be described in good set Victorian terms as the lazy tour of two idle apprentices. For wildness one has to turn to Kinglake's *Eothen*, or Frémont's *Report of the Exploring Expedition to the Rocky Mountains*, or Parkman's *The California and Oregon Trail*, or Melville's *Typee*, all more or less contemporary with the *Week*. Thoreau's harmless camp-outs contrast sharply with Bartram's desperate struggle to preserve his boat and his gear from alligators in eighteenth-century Florida.

The *Week* is no worse for not recording dangers of scalping by Indians or being imprisoned by fanatical Bedouins or being eaten by cannibals, but it is as it is, a volume diversified with essays on Chaucer, local history, the nature and function of poetry, the working of friendship, the nature of time, the truth of Neo-Platonism, a whimsical theory of deserts, the effects of music upon the soul, Huguenots on Staten Island, Pythagoreanism, and the literary style of Sir Walter Raleigh.

I am not trying to find fault with the *Week;* I am merely trying to define its warm humanity, which has only a secondary relation to natural philosophy, as one will realize if he compares it to Muir's *The Mountains of California*, or Clarence King's *Mountaineering in the Sierra Nevada*, or even the far more domesticated *King Solomon's Ring* of Konrad Lorenz, in all of which scientific considerations are vertebrate, and central to the prose.

It has been remarked that Wordsworth does not read very convincingly in the tropics; and when Henry Thoreau had really to confront the savagery of Nature, even in a

relatively limited degree, he found that the warm human-
ism he could impute to natural sights and sounds in east-
ern Massachusetts was not universal or relevant. Nothing
is more illuminating than the mood of cosmic bewilder-
ment that overcame him after his ascent of Mount Ktaadn,
as recorded in *The Maine Woods:*

> Some part of the beholder, even some vital part, seems to
> escape through the loose grating of his ribs as he ascends.
> He is more lone than you can imagine. There is less of
> substantial thought and fair understanding in him than in
> the plains where men inhabit. His reason is dispersed and
> shadowy, more thin and subtile, like the air. Vast, Titanic,
> inhuman Nature has got him at disadvantage, caught him
> alone, and pilfers him of some of his divine faculty. She
> does not smile on him as in the plains. She seems to say
> sternly, Why came ye here before your time. . . . This
> ground is not prepared for you. . . . The tops of the
> mountains are among the unfinished parts of the globe,
> whither it is a slight insult to the gods to climb and pry
> into their secrets, and try their effect on our humanity.
> Only daring and insolent men, perchance, go there. Sim-
> ple races, as savages, do not climb mountains—their tops
> are sacred and mysterious tracts never visited by them.

And, some six pages later:

> This was that Earth of which we have heard, made out of
> Chaos and Old Night. Here was no man's garden, but
> the unhandseled globe. It was no lawn, nor pasture, nor
> mead, nor woodland, nor lea, nor arable, nor waste land.
> It was the fresh and natural surface of the planet Earth,
> as it was made forever and ever. . . . Man was not to be
> associated with it. It was Matter, vast, terrific—not his
> Mother Earth that we have heard of, nor for him to tread
> on, or to be buried in,—no, it were being too familiar even
> to let his bones lie there,—the, home, this, of Necessity
> and Fate.

There is more to the passage, all in the same tone. This,
clearly, is not cosmic comfort but cosmic scare. It suggests that for Thoreau, as for Wordsworth, Nature is in

the temperate zone, never far from the clearing, and has its meaning principally in terms of man.

Man is rather more central to Thoreau's interest, despite the endless pages of natural lore in the *Journal,* than some schools of interpretation are prepared to admit. This truth is the more strongly suggested when we contrast some of the books brought out within three or four years of his death with the four volumes of extracts on nature from the *Journal* published by H. G. O. Blake about a quarter of a century afterward. Thus, *A Yankee in Canada* is virtually a sociological report on French-Canadian life; and not even Thoreau's curiosity about the falls in the rivers of Canada dislocates the centrality of the theme of Canadian culture.

The Maine Woods has, I think, two major interests, one of which is the actual life of white man and red man in the woods or in the clearings, and the processes of their existence; and the other is Indian psychology, especially the psychology of Joseph Polis, of which the "Allegash and East Branch" section of the book is a lengthy exposition in biographical form.

Thoreau's interest in processes is an important element in the volume. A long passage on the New England Friction Match Company, a description of the McCauslin clearing, the way Joe Polis killed, skinned, and cut up a moose, the account of the Ansel Smith place, the way the guide set up camp, the way Joe Polis carried a canoe, the way Henry Thoreau located his lost companion—these passages of circumstantial observation of human behavior make us understand why, two thirds of the way through the book, Thoreau writes:

> Wild as it was, it was hard for me to get rid of the association of the settlements. Any deadly and monotonous sound, to which I did not distinctly attend, passed for a sound of human industry. The waterfalls which I heard were not without their dams and mills to my imagination,—and

several times I found that I had been regarding the steady rushing sound of the wind from over the woods beyond the rivers as that of a train of cars,—the cars of Quebec.

Even his magnificent description of the desolation wrought by flooding a lake draws from him a civic comparison to the "wharves of the largest city in the world, decayed, and the earth and planking washed away," just before they reach the safe haven of the Chamberlain farm.

As for that remarkable book, *Cape Cod*, who can forget the human drama of the shipwreck at Cohasset, the vivid account of the Wellfleet oysterman and his family, the memorable descriptions of Provincetown, or the shrewd remark that the Pilgrims possessed few of the qualities of the pioneer: "They did not go at once into the woods with their axes. They were a family and a church, and were more anxious to keep together, though it were on the sand, than to explore and colonize a New World." Thoreau's book is a close examination of how it is possible to live in an area so barren that the author several times "refrained from asking the inhabitants for a string or a piece of wrapping-paper, for fear I should rob them." The landscape, or rather the seascape, is wonderfully described, but the problem is the environment as a setting for human existence, not, as on the top of Mount Ktaadn, the landscape as a denial of human validity.

One is grateful for serious studies of Thoreau and Transcendentalism, Thoreau and Oriental thought, Thoreau and the classics, Thoreau and the Harvard library, Thoreau and politics. I venture to suggest, however, that the topic of Thoreau and human nature is still a central theme.

There is a wonderful episode in Volume Five of the *Journal* (the entry is dated May 31, 1853), in which Thoreau tries to get George Melvin to tell him where he found the *Azalea nudiflora*, which reads as if it were written in prose by Robert Frost. George Melvin was not going to give in easily; whereupon Thoreau said, "Well, I told him he had better tell me where it was; I was a botanist and ought to know." Channing had almost stumbled upon the secret place but hadn't found it, and the entry runs: " 'Channing,' he said 'came close by it once, when it was in flower. He thought he'd surely find it then; but he didn't, and he said nothing to him.' "

Melvin, Thoreau, and the dog finally go to the spot. We have this characteristic bit of Yankee psychology:

> Melvin showed me how near Channing came. ("You won't tell him what I said; will you?" said he.) I offered to pay him for his trouble, but he wouldn't take anything. He had just as lief I'd know as not. He thought it first came out last Wednesday, on the 25th.

Or take this wonderful description of the drunken Dutchman in the *Journal* for 1850, which I condense:

> Getting into Patchogue late one night in an oysterboat, there was a drunken Dutchman aboard whose wit reminded me of Shakespeare. When we came to leave the beach, our boat was aground, and we were detained three hours waiting for the tide. In the meanwhile two of the fishermen took an extra dram at the beach house. Then they stretched themselves on the seaweed by the shore in the sun to sleep off the effects of their debauch. One was an inconceivably broad-faced Dutchman,—but oh! of such a peculiar breadth and heavy look. I should not know whether to call it more ridiculous or sublime. . . . For the whole voyage they lay flat on their backs on the bottom of the boat, in the bilge-water and wet with each bailing, half insensible and wallowing in their vomit. But ever and anon, when aroused by the rude kicks or curses of the skipper, the Dutchman, who never lost his wit nor equanimity, though snoring and rolling in the vomit produced by his debauch, blurted forth some happy repartee like an illuminated swine. It was the earthiest, slimiest wit I ever heard. The countenance was one of a million. . . . When we were groping up the narrow creek of Patchogue at ten o'clock at night, keeping our boat off, now from this bank, now from that . . . the two inebriates roused them-

selves betimes. . . . The Dutchman gave wise directions
to the steerer. . . . Suddenly rousing himself up where
the sharpest-eyed might be bewildered in the darkness,
he leaned over the side of the boat and pointed straight
down into the creek, averring that the identical hole was
a first-rate place for eels. And again he roused himself at
the right time and declared what luck he had once had
with his pots . . . in another place, which we were floating
over in the dark. At last he suddenly stepped on to another
boat which was moored to the shore, with a divine ease
and sureness, saying, "Well, good-night, take care of yourselves, I can't be with you any longer." He was one of the
few remarkable men whom I have met. . . . When I said,
"You have had a hard time of it to-day," he answered with
indescribable good humor out of the midst of his debauch,
with watery eyes, "Well, it doesn't happen every day."

We rub our eyes. Is this the Henry Thoreau who sought
in vain for a hound, a bay-horse, and a turtledove, or is it
a picture by Hogarth or Teniers sympathetically translated
out of pigment into prose?

Our histories of American literature are deficient in a
number of categories. They seldom or never, for example,
recognize the greatness of American biographical writing,
which, beginning before Cotton Mather and extending to
our own time, has given us masterpieces by James Parton,
Gamaliel Bradford, Douglas Southall Freeman, and others.
They scarcely know what to do with most nonfictional
prose, whether of the informal essay type, of political
theory, or of science; and to read in them one would in
many cases never learn that writers like Samuel Leonard,
Daniel Dulany, John C. Calhoun, or Herbert Croly in one
category, or James Wilson, Matthew Fontaine Maury, Isaac
Ray, or Louis Agassiz in another, ever lived in the United
States.

They do not know what to do with the powerful library
of travel literature written by Americans like John C.
Fremont, John Wesley Powell, Isaac L. Stevens, Frederick
Law Olmsted, or George B. Catlin—books that are cata-

logued in these histories but never analyzed as works of literary art. But I think the greatest deficiency in these manuals is their failure to recognize the existence of that type of writer the French call the moralist. For him American literary criticism has small space.

With us the moral is always equated with the didactic; and, properly, we flee from writing that has too palpable a design upon us. But the great moralists of the ancient world, like Cato, Theophrastus, and Plutarch; the great moralists of Europe—Machiavelli, Montaigne, La Rochefoucauld, Pascal, Lichtenberg, Voltaire, Vauvenargues; and our own Franklin and Emerson are not thus childishly to be dismissed.

When Pascal writes, "Men never do evil so completely and cheerfully as when they do it from religious conviction"; when Voltaire writes, "I never made but one prayer to God, a very short one: 'O Lord, make my enemies ridiculous.' And God granted it"; when Emerson writes, "I have heard with admiring submission the experience of the lady who declared that the sense of being perfectly well-dressed gives a feeling of inward tranquility which religion is powerless to bestow," we know in each case that we are in the hands of someone who has profound observations to make about human nature. Such *sententiae* are not epigrams in the modern sense, though they may be in the classical meaning of the term, and they rise above mere brilliance in proportion as they make us feel their authors are men of sagacity, writers who have seen

> cities of men
> And manners, climates, councils, governments,

themselves not least, but honored of them all. They have probed motives, analyzed actions, distinguished between the specious and the real; and they have been led to their generalizations partly by the love of an art that prefers condensation to expansiveness, and partly by a passionate interest in human character.

Thoreau is one of the great moralists in the French sense. In his apothegms, his pithy paragraphs on human behavior, we more frequently find that quality Lowell praised in Thoreau's writing: "The style is compact and the language has an antique purity like wine grown colorless with age." He labored to perfect this lapidary effect. In 1851 in the *Journal* he spoke of "sentences uttered with your back to the wall," and the next year he said: "The peculiarity of a work of genius is the absence of the speaker from his speech." A little before he quit his journal he wrote: "The fruit a thinker bears is *sentences,—*statements or opinions." Sententiousness—the creating of the rhetorical form known as the *sententia*—is, I think, one of the unique achievements in Thoreau. Whereas his pages on Nature tend to be loose and repetitive, his writing about man is tight and condensed. We have had a small library of books on Nature out of Thoreau; we lack a good book on human nature in Thoreau.

I find the key of this writing in an entry for June 15, 1840, in the *Journal:*

> Why always insist that men incline to the moral side of their being? Our life is not all moral. Surely, its actual phenomena deserve to be studied impartially. The science of Human Nature has never been attempted, as the science of Nature has. The dry light has never shone on it. Neither physics nor metaphysics have touched it.

It is not necessary to determine whether this is a transcendental remark in order to comprehend the special quality of Thoreau as an observer of humanity.

The subject is difficult for the critic to handle because all our attempts to force Thoreau into a system are as futile as the same attempt is with respect to Montaigne or La

Rochefoucauld. Consider, however, these striking *sententiae* culled from the pages of Thoreau's *Journal:*

> Man is the artificer of his own happiness.
> The words of some men are thrown forcibly against you and adhere like burrs.
> We may well neglect many things, provided we overlook them.
> Nothing was ever so unfamiliar and startling to me as my own thoughts.
> The man of principle never gets a holiday.
> There must be some narrowness in the soul that compels one to have secrets.
> Any reverence, even for a material thing, proceeds from an elevation of character.
> The imagination never forgives an insult.

Each of these compels one to think. But to what system of thought shall they be referred?

Sometimes Thoreau's *sententiae* have a Voltairean tone, as in the following:

> Read the Englishman's history of the French and Indian wars, and then read the Frenchman's, and see how each awards the meed of glory to the other's monsters of cruelty or perfidy.
> One man lies in his words, and gets a bad reputation; another in his manners, and enjoys a good one.
> Beauty and true wealth are always thus cheap and despised. Heaven, or paradise, might be defined as the place which men avoid.

I am tempted to put into the same category this startling sentence:

> I should be pleased to meet man in the woods. I wish he were to be encountered like wild caribous and moose.

This is perhaps superficial cynicism. Deeper lie more searching meditations on man that to me, at least, are quite as good as anything in La Rochefoucauld. Here are two:

> No innocence can quite stand up under suspicion, if it is conscious of being suspected. In the company of one

who puts a wrong construction upon your actions, they are apt really to deserve a mean construction. While in that society I can never retrieve myself. Attribute to me a great motive, and I shall not fail to have one; but a mean one, and the fountain of virtue will be poisoned by the suspicion.

It is only by a sort of voluntary blindness, and omitting to see, that we know ourselves, as when we see stars with the side of the eye. . . . It is as hard to see one's self as to look backwards without turning round. And foolish are they that look in glasses with that intent.

The component of stoicism in Thoreau's outlook has been much discussed. Stoicism is an ambiguous word, but I have been struck by passage after passage in the *Journal* that expresses the temper of Marcus Aurelius in the *Meditations*. Here are two representative instances:

Nature refuses to sympathize with our sorrow. She seems not to have provided for, but by a thousand contrivances against, it. She has bevelled the margins of the eyelids that the tears may not overflow on the cheek.

If I have brought this weakness on my lungs, I will consider calmly and disinterestedly how the thing came about, that I may find out the truth and render justice. Then, after patience, I shall be a wiser man than before.

Possibly should be put under this rubric what is to me the saddest line in all Thoreau:

The bones of children soon turn to dust again.

The observation is, if you will, commonplace, but it comes from a childless man who hungered on his deathbed for the companionship of the young.

But the *sententiae* are not confined to the sad sincerity of the great Roman; they also have the warmth, humor, and vitality of Montaigne. Some of the passages on men of the ancient world might have been written by that essayist. For example:

The Greeks were boys in the sunshine, the Romans were

men in the field, the Persians women in the house, the
Egyptians old men in the dark.

And finally, I cite this remarkable piece of self-analysis:

> I only know myself as a human entity, the scene, so to
> speak, of thoughts and affections, and am sensible of a
> certain doubleness by which I can stand as remote from
> myself as from another. However intense my experience,
> I am conscious of the presence and criticism of a part of
> me, which, as it were, is not a part of me, but spectator,
> sharing no experience, but taking note of it, and that is
> no more I than it is you. When the play—it may be the
> tragedy of life—is over, the spectator goes his way. It
> was a kind of fiction, a work of the imagination only, so
> far as he was concerned.

These are, of course, but samplings of about four hundred *sententiae* from the *Journal* alone. More could be
found in the formal books. I have cited nothing from
Thoreau's sardonic observations on New England church
life, on politicians, on family relationships, on the structure and manners of society, on science, or on the races
of men, though I think the following too interesting to
omit:

> There is always a slight haze or mist on the brow of an
> Indian. The white man's brow is clear and distinct. It
> is eleven o'clock in the forenoon with him. It is four
> o'clock in the morning with the Indian.

In categorizing many of the passages I have quoted as
being like Voltaire or La Rochefoucauld, Marcus Aurelius
or Montaigne, I wish neither to enter into a dreary debate over literary sources nor to derogate from the origi-
nality of Thoreau. I am merely trying to define him and to
celebrate an aspect of his genius that seems to me
neglected. Were we to extract from his writing the *sententiae* he wrote on human nature, human conduct, and
human psychology, number them, and print them as separate paragraphs (as some of his observations on nature

have been printed), we should have a book like the *Maximes* of La Rochefoucauld, the *Pensées* of Pascal, and the aphorisms of Lichtenberg.

We ought to restore this surveyor of Concord to his rightful place as a shrewd and candid observer of the motives and behavior of men. He observed humanity quite as objectively as he did the muskrat and the loon. The moralist does not have to be tied to a system. It is enough, as Louis Kronenberger has said, that he gaze back and forth between his fellow beings and himself. Thoreau, I repeat, is, in the French sense, one of the great moralists of the Western world.

Living
Is So Dear

The story of Thoreau's life is well known. He was born, he lived out his life, and he died after forty-four years in Concord, Massachusetts. He travelled extensively in New England and occasionally lectured in other parts of the country. He made pencils, taught school, did some surveying—though, as he said, it often spoiled his feeling for the woods, for he knew where the sticks were hidden marking out the ownership. He was most interested, however, in something quite different—in learning how to live in confronting his friends and neighbors with his thoughts and with the challenge of his life! He was a friend and disciple of Emerson, and though in his writing he produced far less in volume, what he produced was far sharper in its power to penetrate the problems of that age and ours. He kept a journal to record his thoughts, and in that there is such a wealth of stimulation that man to this hour has not begun to mine it out.

He spent two years and two months in a cabin which he himself had built on the shore of Walden Pond in Concord where he prepared the material for the book upon which his fame is founded. That book, as well as his other writings and journal, contains an indictment of human civilization and a warning of where it is taking man that stands unparalleled in precision and penetration. It contains as well a challenge, a summons, a call to a better way of life which Henry Thoreau was prepared, not only to preach, but also to pioneer.

The essence of Thoreau's indictment of civilization was that in it and by it man had been tripped and trapped into substituting earning a living for living itself. This has led him to become less and less the master and more and more the slave of his passion for things. Instead of spending his time in observation and reflection, in conversation and communion with Nature and neighbor, in self-understanding and growth, in social concern and development, he was spending it working to accumulate unworthy things—houses, fields, barns, cattle, furniture— a great many more than any man could use or need. He had become their slave.

Instead of having more time, man found himself with less and less time. Everything was hurry and worry, and he seldom knew what it meant to have inner peace. He was trapped by his possessions. "When the farmer," he wrote, "has got his house, he may not be the richer but the poorer for it, and it may be the house that has got him." Or again, "Beware of all enterprises that require new clothes and not a new wearer of clothes." "All men want," he wrote, "not something to do with, but something to do, or rather something to *BE*." Here is existentialism a hundred years before Tillich! "A man is rich," he wrote, "in proportion to the number of things which he can afford to let alone."

Thoreau was critical of man's enslavement to speed and motion and his increasing attraction for travel. A man does not become wise, he said, according to the amount of ground he is able to cover. Quite the contrary, continuous travel would guarantee that he would know nothing deeply—he would never penetrate beneath the surface of life at all. There is no more amusing passage in *Walden* than his careful argument proving that one could get to Fitchburg from Concord faster by walking than by riding the railroad. It all depended upon what one was supposed to be doing in life, even on the way to Fitchburg.

He foresaw a mechanized, impersonal, slave man coming in the future, a man imprisoned in civilization's tomb! His challenge, his call, was to abandon this—to simplify one's wants and one's activities so as to have time, time to live now, in this ripe moment between the two eternities of yesterday and tomorrow, time to be aware of the beauty on every hand and of the wisdom in Nature and in human nature. "To love wisdom," he wrote "is to live according to its dictates a life of simplicity, independence, magnanimity and trust." His own life was a kind of carefully planned rebuke to all those around him who were merely running around earning a living.

Henry Thoreau was no lover of railroads. He saw little use in getting about more rapidly when the real business of life was getting inside one's own soul. For him a locomotive was a kind of symbol of the enslavement, ultimately, of the human spirit. In *Walden* he wrote with fine irony, "If we do not get out sleepers and forge rails, but go to tinkering upon our lives to improve them, who will build railroads? And if railroads are not built, how shall we get to heaven?" And then with scorn, "We do not ride upon the railroad, it rides upon us. Did you ever think what those sleepers are that underlie the railroad? Each one is a man. An Irish man, or a Yankee man. The rails are laid on them and they are covered with sand and the cars run smoothly over them. They are sound sleepers, I assure you." Nor did he approve of the noise of the panting, puffing engine as it pulled the cars by the corner of Walden Pond disturbing his sleep at night.

But I think Thoreau might have approved of some of the crossing signs on that old Fitchburg line of the Boston and Maine. I remember well the sign at the crossing at Waltham Highlands where I was brought up. It is still there: "stop, look, listen!" and somebody had added,

"AND LIVE!" Good advice, in more ways than one. Thoreau would have seen a grim irony in it—that the warning at the crossing might have a double meaning and a deeper one than those who placed it there had dreamed.

I think he would have liked the sign at the next crossing up the line beyond the Waltham Highlands crossing—a dangerous, untended, grade crossing which the train approached around a curve, whistling day and night, with a fine disregard for man's rest. The sign at that crossing was designed for the days when locomotives were locomotives, and when the crosser might well be a horse and wagon. "LOOK OUT FOR THE ENGINE!" it cried. Good advice again, Henry Thoreau would have said, and again in more ways than one.

If he could speak to us today, after a hundred years, what would he say? I have a notion it would be along the lines of "Stop, Look, Listen, and Live!" and perhaps "Look Out for the Engine!" STOP! First of all he would be appalled at the progress we have made in a hundred years toward the complete mechanization of man and his life. Not only have we substituted earning a living for living, but what we are often willing to do to earn it would have nauseated him. We have also substituted maintaining the national pride and economy for safeguarding human life itself upon this planet. We are abandoning our small towns and their face-to-face communities, and are rushing pell mell into the maw of the huge megalopolis. And why? For overweaning desire of those very things that Thoreau warned us so carefully against.

What of life in the megalopolis? How often it is mean and menacing. Some of you have read the study of mental health in midtown Manhattan: twenty-four per cent sick enough to have their functioning impaired; fifty-eight per cent more mildly, moderately disturbed; only eighteen per cent well—in the most favored part of the city. Dr. Michaels at New York Hospital, one of the social psychiatrists who did the study, thinking to calm the fears of some of us, announced that we should not be afraid because New York City as such had nothing to do with these percentages. The percentages hold, he said, for the country as a whole—urban and rural. I was not reassured!

On January 3, 1861, Thoreau wrote in his *Journal*, "Thank God men cannot fly yet, and lay waste the sky as well as the earth. We are safe on that side," and then he added, "for the moment!" What would he think of the world today where we supinely allow essentially insane governments—I use the characterization of Eric Fromm—to make a radioactive sewer of the sky itself?

So I think Thoreau would say, "Stop! The whole trend of your civilization is in the wrong direction. It is upon things rather than upon life. It is upon machines rather than upon men. It is upon buildings, rather than upon humanity, upon love of power, rather than upon the power of love. It exalts the mass and demeans the man. You are driving yourselves to destruction and your civilization to utter disaster. You are slaves, though you prate of freedom, a freedom you no longer even recognize that you have lost." A hundred years ago and more, Thoreau wrote, "Talk about slavery. It is not the peculiar institution of the South—it exists wherever men are bought or sold, wherever a man allows himself to be made a mere tool, and surrenders his inalienable rights of reason and conscience. This slavery is more complete than that which enslaves the body." Or again, and those of us who watch this city build up into the skies, blotting out the blue of heaven, might read over these words: "Most of the stone that a nation hammers goes towards its tomb only. It buries itself alive. As for the Pyramids, there is nothing to wonder at in them so much as the fact that so many men could be found degraded enough to spend their lives constructing a tomb for some ambitious booby, whom it would have been wiser and manlier to have drowned in the Nile. For my part, I should like to know who in those days did not build them, who were above such trifling."

Or again, "Why should we live with such hurry and waste of life? We are determined to be starved before we are even hungry." "As for work, we haven't any of any consequence. We have the St. Vitus dance, and can't keep our heads still." Or again, in his essay on "Life Without Principle," "Let us consider the way in which we spend our lives. This world is a place of business. What an infinite bustle. I am awakened almost every night by the panting of the locomotive. It interrupts my dreams. There is no Sabbath. It would be glorious to see mankind at leisure for once. It is nothing but work, work, work. . . . I think there is nothing, not even crime, more opposed to poetry, to philosophy, aye, to life itself, than this incessant business."

And as for man's play, and the hunters he saw in the woods around Walden, he simply said, "While it might be fun to shoot a snipe or a woodcock, a man might better be engaged in trying to shoot himself."

Let's face it. With us, earning a living has pre-empted living to the point that we are no longer even aware of it, and no longer remember what true, human living was really like. If Thoreau was right, then our civilization has come a long way down a dead-end road, a blind alley, from which there may not be a way back. In that case, the least we can do is to heed the warning—stop! Evaluate! Think!

His second command would be to look! Look about you, Thoreau would say, and see the real world, the wonderful world that God made, which is there on every side for your enjoyment, your understanding, and your gaining of wisdom. Look upon it. See what your eyes are looking at. Be able to describe it to yourself or to others minutely. Enjoy it! Feast your eyes upon it, upon its line and color, upon its motion, upon its loveliness! Watch the rain come

across a lake; watch the shadows of the clouds upon a
distant mountain; see the shape of the blossom with its
exquisite perfection; watch the animals—see how they
live, and the amazing collaboration of relationships within
their lives. Look upon life and see it, and then look into
it—its history, its makeup, its chemistry! Observe what it
is, as well as how it is, and how you react to it. Look into
it—but also through it so that you find in it some meaning,
some moral, some pattern of universal significance. And
when you walk through a grove of hundred-year-old pines,
see yourself in a cathedral with a pointed arch where the
embracing branches meet, high in the sky, the carpet of
needles under your feet, the dim aisles, the soft light,
the spirit responding in the human breast. Understand!
Let it speak wisdom to your soul. Look upon—look into—
look through—so that you experience as deeply as you can
of the human spirit and the wonder of environing Nature.

His third command would be to LISTEN! The world of
Nature is full of sounds, and those sounds are as telling,
as instructive, and as enjoyable as anything that the eyes
can see. There is a description of an afternoon rainstorm
at Walden that must be an experience that has been shared
by everyone who has ever been alone far out in the country, or in the woods. The sound of the rain coming across
a lake, perhaps on the mountain on the other side first,
and then the change of sound, the different quality as it
strikes the lake and comes marching across the water. Or
the sound of rain on one of those afternoons when it
becomes perfectly quiet early in the afternoon and so dark
that the hermit thrush begins to sing in the quiet, thinking
that it is already night. Then suddenly one hears the first
few patters of the rain, the advance guard of an army
coming through the woods, the sound very softly growing
in intensity until suddenly the outriders are going by
wherever one is sitting; and then the whole army comes
rushing by and one is engulfed in one's little fortress,

waiting breathless as the army inundates him. It finally passes and the sun comes out, and one realizes it is merely an exercise. Listen—listen to the world of Nature, enjoy it, learn from it! Listen to people! Listen to people talk! Every conversation is meaningful; every encounter of the human spirit is precious and an opportunity to learn. Listen to yourself most of all, for you are fearfully and wonderfully made.

Yes, his third command would be to listen—to know how to listen to life and to heed its call to the spirit.

And, finally, he would say LIVE!—the greatest command of all. LIVE! Speaking of his experience at Walden Pond Thoreau wrote: "I LIVED there for two years and two months. At present I am a SOJOURNER in civilized life again." Yet living is so DEAR, so humanly lovely and at once so costly, requiring all that we are if it is to be fully, humanly lovely. How Thoreau could use a word like DEAR and make it mean so much—make it almost new to our ears! Most men do not live dearly; they live lives of quiet desperation. But it is not necessary. One can make living his profession. Perhaps the greatest thing about Thoreau is that once he saw the problem clearly and the danger that overshadowed mankind's development, he dared to speak; he dared to defy the general conventional expectation of him and to exemplify in his life what he believed. He dared to stand all alone—all alone before the contrary opinion and expectation of his family, his friends, and his countrymen! He believed not only in his own capacity, but everyone's capacity to improve his life. "What a man thinks of himself, that it is which determines his fate. I know of no more encouraging fact than the unquestionable ability of man to elevate his life by conscious endeavor. In the long run, men hit only what they aim at. Therefore, though they fail immediately, they had better aim at something high." Such was his call.

Stop, Look, Listen and Live! This is his challenge.

What this means is that Henry Thoreau was first and foremost a great moralist—a moralist in the broadest sense of that word. He just cared so intensely about life and its meaning that he was determined to risk his life for life and to confront his fellowmen with its challenge as he saw it.

This is what I consider the greatest moral confrontation that a man can make.

He was also a writer—indeed a master of all the tools and subtleties of the writer's art. He was a perfectionist for style and wrote and rewrote his pages and paragraphs, weighing each for thrust and impact, and the whole for overall balance. He used simile and metaphor, irony and satire, hyperbole and understatement, paradox and pun with telling power; but he never used them as ends in themselves and never to show off, but always with an overriding moral purpose.

He was a naturalist. He loved the woods and fields, the lakes and the seashore, but he loved them as the natural setting for man's life and the honest, friendly, context for man's main business, which was meaningful living, and not as ends in themselves—though he would never have begrudged any natural life its right to be an end in itself. He certainly did not want to see it exploited, or, as men usually say, "improved" for man's benefit.

He was a reformer who saw the myriad ties binding society together and cared enough to cry aloud against the social sin in which he found his own soul inexorably enmeshed. Indeed, he was not content merely to cry out; he must refuse cooperation with social evil in its most intense form, and from this came one of the most powerful forces of modern times—the concept of civil disobedience, which Gandhi used to set 450 million Indians free, and with which, at this moment in the South, sit-inners and Freedom Riders challenge the social iniquity and inequity of our day. Never was Thoreau, the reformer, more vividly alive than at this moment.

Most of all, he was an exemplar—one to whom life as such was to be counted dearest of all, and he was not going to mistake the menu, the dishes, the table, and the utensils for the meal, as most men do.

Perhaps he would be discouraged if he could see where we have got ourselves today. Despite his having written and lectured, scolded and shouted, refused taxes and gone to jail; despite *Walden* and the *Journal*, have we understood? Have any of us understood? I wonder!

In a sense he was not saying that we must all be off to Walden. He himself stayed only two years and two months. He was saying we can simplify our wants. We can concentrate upon developing the spiritual qualities of our lives. This option is always open for man, and the call may come again, again, and again—if we have ears to hear!

RAYMOND ADAMS

Thoreau's Claim to Greatness

There are good rules concerning eligibility for election to the Hall of Fame for Great Americans that preclude a man's being present when his name is added to the roll. His life once lived must have been tested by time. But if time did not interfere, Henry Thoreau would not be here. His attitudes are well enough known to make that certain. But contrariety, of which he had a large measure, might bring him even so. If it did, it is pretty certain what he would choose to say. So it is just as well that time and rules and impossibilities stand in the way as firmly as they do.

With all his disdain of diplomas and his dislike of ceremony, Henry Thoreau would not, I am convinced, be surprised in the least that his name is being installed in bronze and his bust is being unveiled today. He might be surprised, as were some among us, that it has taken so many elections before he was chosen for the honor. But that he should be honored here would not surprise him. This would be true because he had so high an idea of what fame is. He was sure fame would ultimately and inevitably cleave to the great life. And the great life was the one which had worked its way "down through the mud and slush of opinion and prejudice" until it stood on the bedrock of truth and could be measured by that "realometer" which he had projected. With confident Transcendentalism, he felt that recognition would flow toward reality and truth. And it had been the business of his whole life to seek that bedrock. First and last, he had no doubt that he had found it. His certainty in this arose as an inner conviction that was Transcendental and that included an equal certainty that truth once announced would draw to itself agreement and accord.

Surely we must give high place to Thoreau's Transcendentalism. That philosophy informed his neighborhood, his acquaintance, and his time. Better yet, it informed his life. I have called it a confident Transcendentalism because he seems never to have had any doubts about it. He did not defend his trust in an "inward morning" nor argue the validity of "higher laws." This may have been partly because he was late on the Transcendental scene and arrived from college when the debate over Transcendentalism was nearly finished—but not entirely finished. He was not a recruit in the pamphlet war that broke out next year over Mr. Emerson's Divinity School Address. That was a theological war. The participants were carefully selected; every combatant was a chaplain. Thoreau was hardly eligible. But it is not enough to say that after college he had only to accept a ready-made philosophy. To say it is to confute it; he did not live his life that way. Moreover, people did debate Transcendentalism, if only within themselves, during the forties and fifties. Emerson most surely did. Thoreau did not. He hardly mentioned it by name, while he lived it implicitly. His early poems are statements of it, and his "Plea for Captain John Brown" together with the essays readied in his last year—"Walking," "Life Without Principle," and "Night and Moonlight" —are equally instinct with it. His life was lived by it in rare moments of mystic communion with the infinite and in almost daily convictions that intuitions of truth were very truth. This is so persistent a quality in the man, so wholehearted, so unquestioned by him, so heeded whether it sent him to the woods of Walden or to the bell rope in

Concord Center on the night of John Brown's execution, that we can claim him as the American Transcendentalist.

Like all Transcendentalists he felt, of course, that no man need look farther than within himself to discover truth no matter where he stood on the face of the earth. But he himself stood in the town of Concord and was satisfied there. We must not forget Concord. He led there one of the happiest lives ever lived in America. And this was not because all Concord admired him or understood him. The townspeople most certainly did not. One of them said he heard five hundred people in Concord damn Henry late in 1859 when he proposed the John Brown memorial meeting; fifteen years earlier even a larger number had damned him for burning a hundred acres of prime woodland rising up from Fair Haven Bay. Within two years after his John Brown action he was praised; but those charred sticks from the fire smudged his reputation in Concord for two generations. He was not happy in Concord because he was understood; he was happy because there he could be his own man better perhaps than in any other town in America, and this because a few people in the town did understand him—Mr. Emerson, Mr. Alcott, Ellery Channing, Edmund Hosmer, the entire "Walden Pond Association," together with his loyal family. His family had at great cost managed to send Henry to college, and afterward they uttered not one word of criticism about a Transcendental way of life that could hardly have been approved by an artisan father and a hard working neighborly mother. Whether they approved or not, they seem to have understood Henry and drew him closer into their little circle as it was narrowed by death. Besides the human quality of the town, Concord offered an ideal countryside for this naturalist. In reckoning up the influences on Thoreau, we must include the physical town of Concord, as good for his purposes as two centuries before it had been for Bulkeley, Hunt, Willard, Hosmer, Meriam, Flint, when they saw the land lying fair to the south and said in Emerson's line, "This suits me for a pasture; that's my park."

Within that little town he lived his life and wrote his books, for once he was home from college, his absences from Concord were mere excursions. The incidents of his life that are known wherever men know our literature are incredibly simple even for one who said, "Let your affairs be as two or three." Chiefly his were three: he was locked in jail for one night; he lived for twenty-six months in a little house on the shore of Walden Pond less than a mile from home; and he was for all his years romantically and scientifically concerned with the natural history of Concord, measuring what he found in the Maine Woods or on Cape Cod or at last along the rivers of Minnesota by whether it was to be found in Concord also. These are the things everyone knows about Henry Thoreau—little enough unless genius amend them.

One night in jail for not paying a tax of a dollar or two was surely not an impressive detention. But he made that jailing representative of a free man's compact with his government, with all government, raising the individual above the state, and then wrote an account of the event that has caught the imagination of people ever since. Not long ago it taught Mahatma Gandhi how to resist imperialism and make India free; and just now it is teaching Freedom Riders and sit-in demonstrators how to make American states abandon inhumane laws and customs. The century since the jailing has seen unbelievable tyrannies arise to put the state above the individual. But in their way has stood the principle of civil resistance which Henry Thoreau voiced for us all.

When he was less than thirty years old, he built for himself a one-room house on the shore of Walden Pond, living there hardly more than two years, not doing anything spectacular, not even satisfying the gossips by being a model recluse or hermit. The villagers did think he was a bit eccentric. And they still thought so after he tried to explain his actions in some lectures before the village lyceum and even after he wrote the book *Walden*. But people since then have not dismissed it as an eccentricity. The book has appeared in a hundred editions and been translated into all the major languages of the world. That is because Thoreau tied his experiment in living at the pond to another fundamental principle: how a man can simplify his life and be himself in the face of the complexities and involvements and pressures of Western society. He didn't think that everyone should live a life in the woods, but rather that everyone should make sure that the life he was living was really life. Since then the entanglements of living have made the complexities of his day seem simple in comparison. But each new complication has only intensified the human longing to get beyond involvement and arrive at lives of single purpose and integrity. So, in a mechanizing world, each new generation has been able to consider *Walden* written quite as much to its condition as to that of the generation which saw the publication of the book.

There remains the most pervasive fact of all, his life in nature, from the youthful zest of being outdoors to a scientific observation and reporting of natural history, through to a sympathy and ecstatic love which made him a familiar of the morning that brought the heroic ages and of the sunset over a Concord level in which "nothing was wanting to make a paradise of that meadow" and of the night "with its dews and darkness came to restore the drooping world." He lived in nature so deeply, met it and invited it in so many moods, observed it or absorbed it with such keen sensitivity that it is impossible in a sentence to estimate this factor of his life. He was not unjustly called by his contemporary a poet-naturalist, nor was he any the less valuable to the less sentimental naturalist of the next generation. Perhaps his great contribution as a naturalist was pointing out to his time and to ours the worth of wildness itself in the economy of human life.

His going to jail declared the right of the individual man against the State. His going to Walden spoke for people who find themselves increasingly encompassed by "improved means to unimproved ends." But his going to the wild speaks especially to our time when the growth of cities and suburbs and the crowding of the earth everywhere threatens to take wildness from us and has made the little of it we can keep precious, indeed, not only for conservation and recreation but for satisfying a primal hunger within us. These are the claims to greatness which found their timeless statement in the beautiful books of Henry Thoreau.

BRAJ KUMAR NEHRU

Henry David Thoreau: A Tribute

On the 6th of May, 1862, Henry David Thoreau was laid to rest where he had spent the major part of his life—in the wooded hills of his beloved Concord. One hundred years later, we gather in this vast metropolis to do him honour and to inscribe his name in the Hall of Fame. It is a recognition of the essential permanence of Thoreau's teachings; it is equally a recognition that, as recently reported in a celebrated American newspaper, "The ideas of an eccentric Yankee individualist . . . have spun round the world and have provided the oppressed with an honourable philosophy of resistance."

We wish to pay homage to the memory of a man who, drawing from the ancient Indian scriptures their prescription for the dignity of the human soul, in turn postulated the status in political society of what Professor Laski was later to call "that last inwardness of the human mind which resists all authority save its own conviction of rectitude." There are between our two countries many bonds that will endure the test of time. There are the shared beliefs in the ideals so eloquently set forth in your Declaration of Independence. There is the common belief in the rights of man and the dignity of the individual. There is the shared passion for the democratic way of life and for the establishment of a peaceful and just world order. But there is also a deep relationship between the thinking of Concord in the last century and the shape of India today. Thoreau had in his library a number of books on Indian philosophy, and the development of his thought was obviously affected by them. That thought, in turn, had the profoundest effect on Mahatma Gandhi, the maker of modern India, and is consequently today one of the elements that make up our national consciousness. Gandhiji himself acknowledged freely and often his having drawn on Thoreau's individual and social philosophy. He conveyed to President Roosevelt in July, 1942, how deeply influenced he had been by Thoreau's writings. In an open letter to the American people at about the same time, he wrote: "You have given me a teacher in Thoreau who furnished me through his essay on "The Duty of Civil Disobedience" scientific confirmation of what I was doing." It is, therefore, in the fitness of things that I, as the Ambassador of Gandhiji's country, come here to pay tribute to the spirit of Thoreau.

It is one of the great paradoxes—and equally redeeming features—of human history and evolution that as the scale of organised society grows and as the gregariousness and enveloping nature of that society increasingly dominates the individual, the very same process highlights the extreme individuality of the human conscience. The more the conformist nature of society grows, the more accented is the nonconformity of what the ancient Hindus called the "atman"—the individual soul. It is the spirit of nonconformity that has enriched the dialogue of human progress—no less, indeed, in the material fields than in the spiritual. The blooming of many flowers in ancient Chinese thought; the periodic enrichment of Hindu philosophy by great men like the Buddha and Shankaracharya; the resurgence of the human spirit heralded by Jesus Christ; the reformatory movements within the Christian church in Europe following the Dark Ages; the enlivening of political thought first in Europe, then in this country, and later in the erstwhile colonial empires, that led to the overthrow of conformity to an authoritarian or alien rule—all of these analysed to their fundamentals are basic proof of the moving force of individual conscience and of the role that it can play in uprooting existing order if such order be unrighteous.

Thoreau and Gandhiji were two great nonconformists. Thoreau lived and worked in a country whose political testament was based on the right of people to resist arbitrary power. As a grand jury in Georgetown, South Carolina, declared in 1776:

> When a people . . . find that, by the baseness and corruption of their rulers, those laws which were intended as the guardians of their sacred and inalienable rights, are impiously perverted into instruments of oppression: and, in violation of every social compact, and the ties of common justice, every means is adopted by those whom they instituted to govern and protect them, to enslave and destroy them; human nature and the laws of God justify their imploying those means for redress which self-preservation dictates.

In a country where the powers of government were limited, where arbitrary power was checked, where the approval of the ruled through their legislatures was the sanction for the acts of the rulers, and where there was not the frustrating and desolating aspect of despotic power —as in India—to incite and provoke into revolt the inner sense of rectitude of man, it is somewhat surprising that a Thoreau arose here. And yet he did.

Where and how did Thoreau carry the concept of the duty of disobedience further than was accepted till his time? The exercise of the "right of resistance" was, in the words of Samuel West in 1776, the prerogative of "the publick: not a few disaffected individuals but the collective body of the State." Secondly, where "the overwhelming majority of a thoroughly abused people" felt it necessary, resistance was justified in the sense of armed rebellion—the "appeal to God by the sword" as the colony of New Hampshire termed it. Thirdly, resistance was measured in terms of failure of the government to observe legality either in the sense of adherence to established law or in the sense of having the consent of the governed.

If this understanding of the revolutionary concept of the right of resistance is correct, then Thoreau seems to have carried the idea much further. He measured the sanctity of secular power not in terms of a legal process or of a parliamentary sanction, but in terms of a more deep-seated ethic—namely, the conviction of an abiding rectitude. "The only obligation which I have the right to assume is to do at any time what I think right." The right, and indeed the duty, of disobedience to secular power came to be a moral, and not merely a legal, issue. Further, this was a right that each and every citizen had. It mattered not if he was one of many protestants or was a lonely person whose conscience did not permit him to conform to the political ethics of his society; he had the right to disobey. It would thus seem that Thoreau was defining—or was it redefining?—the context of the individual human sense of values to the outside world.

As Gandhiji pointed out later, such an attitude was something that called for the highest courage, the loftiest conception of freedom. The courage that it calls for is clearly stated in Gandhiji's simple but awesome statement, "The method of passive resistance is the clearest and safest, because, if the cause is not true, it is the resisters, and they alone, who suffer." The conception of freedom that the Thoreauesque attitude entails was perhaps never so clearly stated as by Thoreau himself; from the prison he was able to reflect, "If there was a wall of stone between me and my townsmen, there was a still more difficult one to climb or break through before they could get to be as free as I was." Or, as Gandhiji, in somewhat greater detail, put it:

> An out-and-out civil resister simply ignores the authority of the State. He becomes an outlaw claiming to disregard every unmoral State law. . . . This he does because, and when, he finds the bodily freedom he seemingly enjoys to be an intolerable burden. He argues to himself that a State allows personal freedom only insofar as the citizen submits to its regulations. Submission to the State law is therefore the price a citizen pays for his personal liberty. Submission, therefore, to a State law wholly or largely unjust is an immoral barter for liberty.

And I have no doubt at all that Thoreau would have agreed with Gandhiji when the latter declared:

> My work will be finished if I succeed in carrying conviction to the human family that every man or woman, however weak in body, is the guardian of his or her self-respect and liberty. This defence avails, though the whole world may be against the individual resister.

These high expectations and ideals of the human consciousness, acting as a free and untrammelled entity, may conceivably have joined the limbo of history with other idealist aberrations had it not been for the demonstration in action of how civil disobedience can be every whit as powerful an instrument as armed resistance. The great national movement in India, since it came under the influence of Gandhiji in the second decade of this century, was based on the premise that it was the duty of the individual not to cooperate with evil. Gandhiji was only incidentally a political leader and equally incidentally a nationalist. His passionate concern—like Thoreau's passionate concern—was with the individual and with the obstacles that prevented the individual from living the life of self-respect and liberty which Thoreau's conscience, or Gandhiji's inner voice, wanted him to live. Tracing the obstacles to a good or righteous life in the India of his time, it became obvious to him that the root of the malady lay in the continued existence of a foreign occupation and an alien rule; and he therefore concluded that the people must bend their every nerve for the removal of what he called the "satanic" government which ruled over them. He declared: "It is not so much British guns that are responsible for our subjection as our voluntary cooperation." With an almost frightening strength of individual and national will, Gandhiji saw—to use his own words—that "nations like individuals, could only be made through the agony of the cross and in no other way." The path he indicated was the path of civil disobedience and history records the effect. The magnification of Thoreau's technique a hundred-thousandfold—both in time and in numbers—caused ultimately the collapse of the mightiest empire the world has ever known. Here was a clear demonstration on an immense scale of the practicality of the ideas of Thoreau which his detractors had regarded as so impractical.

It is fitting that we should today once again turn our minds to the simple principles that Thoreau preached, to the value of the simple life that he lived, and his burning and passionate concern for the individual. In this modern world, one-third of humanity has chosen forms of political and social organization which exalt the State so high above the individual as almost to cause one to forget that the latter has any rights or that he is anything but an interchangeable spare part in the vast machinery of production. Even the theory on which these societies are based seems to deny what to Thoreau seemed axiomatic—that social and political organizations have validity only insofar as they can lead to the greater growth of the individual.

Another third of humanity alleges great concern with individual freedom, with the value of the spirit, and with man's relationship to God. The theory of these societies is, however, in great danger of being divorced from its practice. In these societies, as a result of a single-minded pursuit of the material goods of life, the individual is in danger of being forced to subordinate himself not necessarily to the State but certainly to organizations that taken collectively are much vaster and more powerful than himself. This subordination detracts from the individual's freedom and impels him with almost irresistible force to drab uniformity and conformity, not only in action but perhaps also in thought. There seems to be inherent in the modern mechanism for the creation of wealth an increasing tendency to subordinate the individual to the process: to assume that the individual is valuable not because God created him in his image but because he is particularly gifted in the performance of the repetitive motions required for the proper functioning of an assembly line. It is to be hoped that in these societies, with the satiety that wealth can produce, there will be an increasing realization that at some stage there should be liberation, not from the power of the State, but from the power of the machine.

The last third of humanity has not yet made the final choice as to what kind of society it is going to have. This third—the one belonging to the newly independent and economically underdeveloped nations—has many obstacles to overcome before its individuals can hope to live the good life. The prime hurdle of an alien rule has largely been removed: the main obstacle now remaining is the removal of that grinding material poverty which degrades the individual to a point where human values have no meaning. The one great objective of these countries is to remove this poverty as rapidly as they can. The experience of those who have been successful in banishing poverty from their own countries, whether they have adopted the communistic or capitalistic method, seems to show that in either event the individual may well go under. He may become an automaton to be used—either at the bidding of the State or at the bidding of a corporation—as a small cog in an enormous machine over whose destiny, no matter what the theory is, he has no control. In either case, his system of values may well be distorted, and the desire for material goods may be so developed that it tends to overshadow and to dominate the many other, and at least equally valuable, aspects of the human personality. The material requirements for a good life, as Thoreau was never tired of pointing out, are in reality very limited. But the experience of existing societies appears to show that once this appetite for material well-being is created, it tends to feed on itself and leads to an elaboration and complexity of material consumption which is not only unnecessary but actually destructive to the fundamental values of humanity.

The wiser among the new societies may, therefore, legitimately engage themselves in a search to find whether it is possible to get rid on the one hand of the curse of poverty, and to avoid on the other the dangers which concentration on the pursuit of wealth creates. The message of Thoreau is, therefore, valuable to them for it serves as a constant reminder that it shall not profit a man to possess the world if he loses his own soul—that there is an unrelenting conflict between the Transcendentalist and the "Organization man" and that no matter how impressive the external trappings one covers oneself with, what is invaluable in the last resort is the individual.